ANCIENT WEST AFRICAN WOMEN TOPPLED CORNERSTONES

ISLAMIZATION, CHATTEL SLAVE TRADING, COLONIZATION & CHRISTIANIZATION

Dr. Christiana Oware Knudsen
Cand. Phil., DK: Ph.D., UK
Retired Social & Medical Anthropologist

PNEUMA SPRINGS PUBLISHING UK

First Published in 2016 by:
Pneuma Springs Publishing

Ancient West African Women - Toppled Cornerstones

ISBN13: 9781782284154

British Library Cataloguing in Publication Data. A catalogue record for this book is available from the British Library.

Pneuma Springs Publishing
A Subsidiary of Pneuma Springs Ltd.
7 Groveherst Road, Dartford Kent, DA1 5JD.
E: admin@pneumasprings.co.uk
W: www.pneumasprings.co.uk

ACKNOWLEDGEMENTS

First, my sincerest thanks go to one African Priest in Rome who asked me to write a book about how Ancient West African women were affected by North Atlantic chattel slave trading.

This book will be sold to help meet the needs of children admitted into some hospitals in West Africa.

Next, my thanks go to Professor Erik Knudsen, who made a first read-through of the manuscript and gave me his opinion about the subject matter.

I would also like to thank the librarians of the City of Brighton & Hove, in the UK, who helped me with some technical matters.

I thank the Danish artist, Rikke Kolkur Sørensen, who has illustrated the slave traders and their human "commodities".

My sincerest thanks to you all.

DEDICATION

I dedicate this book to all you little Children, the newly arrived souls on this Mother Earth Planet, Children of all skin color, of all races, of all cultures, of all religions, and of all nationalities. Children, always show great respect for your mothers, from whose wombs you have emerged, as well as for your fathers, who have contributed spiritually to your physical development, in accordance with the belief of some of the Ancient West African Tribes. As you grow older, always pray to God for the awareness that will enable you to treat others as you would like them to treat you.

PREFACE

My ancient Akan heritage goes back to the Akan tribe, one of the ethnic matriarchal descent system groups who, in ancient times, migrated from Egypt's Nile Valley to the Ancient Ghana Empire in Western Sudan now West Africa. This Empire is known to have existed between 300 BCE and 1235 CE. It should be noted that, that Ancient Ghana Empire dates back even further than 300 BCE, but this was the period when migrants from the Nile Valley first travelled there, about 300 CE. Later on, this ethnic group was among many others which left the Ghana Empire in the early 13th century, going southwards towards the Guinea Coast to avoid being converted to Islam with its patriarchal descent system. Eventually the Akan, with other ethnic groups, reached the Guinea Coast region. Later, this area experienced the most deadly chattel slave trading in human history, followed by colonization and Christianization by people who, like the chattel slave traders, came from Christian Europe. Later on, part of this area, which was named the "Gold Coast" by the British during its colonization, became modern-day Ghana.

Many years ago, one very old retired school teacher I met while travelling in modern Ghana for my anthropological field research work said to me:

> "We escaped the Arab influence by hopping from the frying pan, that is, escaping Islamization and slave trading by the Arab Muslim Traders, and then we landed into the fire, that is, chattel slave trading, colonization and finally Christianization by Christian Europe."

In 1957, I visited Europe for the first time with my husband, the Danish-English medical doctor Dr. Peder Kristian Kjærulff Knudsen, and our first child. Even though, as a young qualified school teacher, I enjoyed seeing many interesting things in Europe, I was also shocked by an observation that did not please me, regarding European women's position in their societies. I observed that European women were not given the same respect as their men, and therefore were treated differently in many ways. Worse still, I encountered the isolation of old people who, according to my culture, should have been living with their families during their last days on this earth. One African man I met on a bus in London said to me:

"Here in Europe, old people's luxury residences are isolated from their family homes, which makes these residences similar to concentration camps."

Again, I noticed the disrespect shown to women by many young people and men - on buses, on trains, in the shops and in the streets. Some shop assistants would be serving old people, especially old women, while at the same time they would be chatting and laughing with their colleagues, not making eye contact with their old women customers while serving them. Later on, I quickly realized that European men also showed general discriminatory treatment to women in West Africa in many respects after they arrived there. The inhuman treatment suffered by these Africans, especially by women chattel slaves on the Guinea Coast, were actually based on these men's own cultures back home in Christian Europe.

Therefore, when I was recently approached by a big international Christian charity organization for children, asking me to write a book about how West African women were affected in the West African chattel slave trade, which would be sold for children's charity work in West Africa, I accepted with great pleasure. Ironically, chattel slave trading, colonization and Christianization on the Guinea Coast, which were carried out by these civilized Christian Europeans, damaged lives and heritage, particularly of women and children, forever.

This book - short, crisp, and full of serious food for thought - therefore starts with the strange and sad, but extraordinarily interesting, information about the development of women's affairs in ancient West Africa. This area was one of the most interesting parts of Africa, even before the arrival of the Arab Muslim salt, gold and slave traders, as well as the Christian European chattel slave traders. Modern archeological findings have proved that people lived in this area, north and south of the Sahara Desert and right down to the Guinea Coast, thousands of years before the various ethnic groups of people from the Nile valley arrived in the region.

The strangest and most interesting common feature of these numerous migrants was their matriarchal descent systems. These provided clear evidence of the great value placed on women, not as sex objects, but rather as foundation cornerstones for humanity's existence on this planet. The reason for this extraordinary value of ancient West African females has been commented upon and summarized by many ancient West African historical writers, as well as ancient oral historians: it is simply that every human being on this planet, woman or man, has been developed in a woman's womb. Therefore, according to some oral historians of ancient belief systems, the female has been especially created to be not aggressive, but gentle, with special inbuilt loving qualities suitable for the patient upbringing of tiny newly arrived souls, for the continuation of the human species on this planet.

Therefore, this ancient belief goes on to say, the fact that a woman may not be physically strong as a man is for a special and very important purpose. Hence, according to some old oral native historians, the ancient West African men were aware of the Creator God's purpose for women in this dimension, and therefore they always treated females with great respect. Unfortunately, those male foreigners who arrived in ancient West Africa, through their ignorance of God's own sacred purpose for women on this planet created many woes and hardships for females in West Africa, which has lasted even to this day.

Hence, according to some illiterate village women I met in West Africa and during my anthropological research travels many years ago, unfortunately both the Arab Muslims and the European Christians who came to West Africa many centuries ago had no understanding of the Creator God's special purpose for women in general, as well as women in West African societies in particular. According to these village women, when these foreigners arrived centuries ago to find these West African women very powerful and influential, with a complementary existence with their men, they became frightened, and found such power unacceptable.

Again, regarding family systems, according to some of the ancient written and oral histories that I have consulted for this book, before the arrival of Islam and Christianity in West Africa each of these numerous, well-established migrant ethnic groups knew and worshipped the "Creator God", but then approached "IT" (not "Him") through various little gods and spirits. Family ties were also very strong, not only between a man, his wife and their children, but also across extended families, entire clans and societies as a whole. However, according to the written and oral histories I have consulted for this work, these traditions were destroyed by the nature of these new religions. Furthermore, some other great changes were also introduced by these foreigners. Polygamy, for example, was not acceptable before the arrival of the Muslims. In ancient times, before foreigners arrived in the northern part of West Africa, only some of the Kings and Chiefs in those regions practiced polygamy for special reasons, such as for political, ethnic and war alliances. But this practice was abhorred by ordinary citizens.

As argued by most writers of ancient slave-trading history, whose works have been part of the cornerstone of this work, the phenomenon of slavery was found all over the world, including Europe, as well as in ancient West Africa. However, chattel slavery - the practice of treating fellow human beings, especially women slaves, as just "things", as "commodities" or "animals" to be bought was introduced to the Guinea Coast by Christian European slave traders. In the end it was West African women who bore the brunt of this irreparable damage to their existence, and continue to do so right until the present day.

The colonialism which followed this chattel slavery and the introduction of Christianity, all carried out by the same Christian Europeans, finally stamped out the great respect which West African women used to receive from their societies, as well as their complementary respectful existence with their men. Therefore, in West Africa today, the serious issue now for women is the fight for mutual respect from their men through "Emancipation of Women" programs, the same status that Western women are also fighting for today.

Finally, this book is unique as it has been written in a style which combines very carefully selected academic research writing with a carefully chosen, reliable ancient West African "Oral History". Therefore, this work, in some ways, is similar to the way most of those ethnic groups who migrated from the Nile Valley region to the Western Sudan area used to tell their histories. That is, during the week, at sunset, when the people had finished eating their evening meals and the brilliant full moon had appeared, children of all ages, young people, middle-aged people and old people of all ages, would gather in the courtyards of their houses and huts, or

polygamy for special reasons, such as for political, ethnic and war alliances. But this practice was abhorred by ordinary citizens.

As argued by most writers of ancient slave-trading history, whose works have been part of the cornerstone of this work, the phenomenon of slavery was found all over the world, including Europe, as well as in ancient West Africa. However, chattel slavery - the practice of treating fellow human beings, especially women slaves, as just "things", as "commodities" or "animals" to be bought was introduced to the Guinea Coast by Christian European slave traders. In the end it was West African women who bore the brunt of this irreparable damage to their existence, and continue to do so right until the present day.

The colonialism which followed this chattel slavery and the introduction of Christianity, all carried out by the same Christian Europeans, finally stamped out the great respect which West African women used to receive from their societies, as well as their complementary respectful existence with their men. Therefore, in West Africa today, the serious issue now for women is the fight for mutual respect from their men through "Emancipation of Women" programs, the same status that Western women are also fighting for today.

Finally, this book is unique as it has been written in a style which combines very carefully selected academic research writing with a carefully chosen, reliable ancient West African "Oral History". Therefore, this work, in some ways, is similar to the way most of those ethnic groups who migrated from the Nile Valley region to the Western Sudan area used to tell their histories. That is, during the week, at sunset, when the people had finished eating their evening meals and the brilliant full moon had appeared, children of all ages, young people, middle-aged people and old people of all ages, would gather in the courtyards of their houses and huts, or outside underneath huge old trees with huge long thick roots on which people could sit in comfort. Then old women or old men would tell of their history, and sometimes sing songs connected to whatever history they were telling. So, here we go, with the carefully chosen written and oral history of "Ancient West African Women. Toppled Cornerstones".

The information in this book has been carefully researched, and numerous references are included at the end of this book for further reading. I have been careful in choosing my written references, because it is well known that, for example, three historians or travelers may write in completely different ways about something that they experienced together at the same time, giving completely different meanings to the same thing that they experienced together. Many ancient historians and travelers who wrote about West Africa did not take interest in West African women's affairs, due to the patriarchal cultures they came from. The same was true of oral historians who took interest only in the cultures they themselves belonged to. Therefore, the sources of this book have been carefully chosen to make this work reliable, and therefore valuable.

CONTENTS

INTRODUCTION

I have given the nickname "TOPPLED CORNERSTONES" to the powerful ancient West African women, for the simple reason that they were very powerful and clever in many ways and therefore symbolically became natural "foundation cornerstones" on which their tribes and societies were built. Another reason for their extraordinarily powerful influence was the ancient argument in their societies that, since every man on this planet came from a woman's womb, women had to decide what was right for their "babies".

Ancient West Africa was one of the most extraordinary, beautiful and unique places on the African Continent. Unfortunately, as we shall see later, this area has been forever tarnished in many ways, for example by slave-trading activities in that region. These affected women particularly badly, a fact recognized by many historians and non-historians alike, all over the world, with knowledge of the Christian Europe's North Atlantic chattel slave trading.

This type of "commodity" slave trading was initiated by Christian Portugal a few years before 1470, but then many other Christian European countries joined in. These trading activities continued for nearly 400 years, until the beginning of the 19th century, that is, 1807 CE (although the Danish-Norwegian kingdom abolished it a few years earlier). However, even though it was officially abolished by this date, trading from the Guinea Coast of West Africa continued discretely until the late 19th century.[1] This phenomenon is considered the worst tragedy in human existence on this planet so far; a tragedy whose effects can never be erased from human memory.

This phenomenon of chattel slave trading, this tragedy, saw a fellow human being become a "commodity" or a "thing" belonging to another human being, a commodity with no rights and no kin, whose owners could get rid of "it" as they chose. West African Women paid a heavy price for this phenomenon which, paradoxically, became the basis for the development of Christian Western modern civilization and their excessive material wealth.

The destruction of the West African women's unique, powerful matriarchal descent systems was based on the following phenomena: Islamization, chattel slave trading, colonization and Christianization. These were then followed by the contemporary globalization of Western materialist values, which have also spread to West Africa, destroying forever the already weakened heritage of West African women's power.

Before we examine some details of the aforementioned phenomena and their tragic influence on matriarchal descent systems in West Africa, we will first briefly summarize the origins of ancient West African empires and kingdoms. Next, we will describe the roles played by West African women in their societies, which made them solid cornerstones for society in those days. We shall then briefly consider the beginning of the end of these women's statuses as cornerstones, as foreign influence introduced patriarchal descent systems. Finally, we will also examine the everlasting tragic effects on West African women of the North Atlantic chattel slave trade, Islamization, colonization, and finally, Christianization.

Picture 1: The Talking Drums At An Akan Festival

PART 1

CHAPTER 1

A BRIEF LOOK AT THE ORIGINS OF ANCIENT WEST AFRICAN EMPIRES AND KINGDOMS

Ancient West Africa has long been a very interesting part of Africa. It was divided into two sections centuries ago, initially by foreign invading Arab Muslims: salt, gold and slave traders and their scholars. These Muslims termed the area from the north coast of West Africa to the Sahara desert, "Bilad al Bidan', that is, "Land of the Whites", and the area south of the Sahara desert down to the Guinea Coast, "Bilad as Sudan", that is, "Land of the Blacks".(2)

Later on, both Christian Europeans and Muslim Arabs called the area extending from the Southern Sahara south to the Atlantic Ocean, the "Western Sudan" (modern-day West Africa). This area was rich in empires, nations and kingdoms; it had rivers, streams and lakes, stretching from the southern part of the Sahara Desert, across the Savannah's south to the shores of the Atlantic Ocean, that is, the Guinea Coast.

Among the groups of people who lived in the "Western Sudan" was the Akan kingdom, one of the many ethnic groups who migrated from the Nile Valley into the powerful ancient Ghana Empire in that region. Other kingdoms and empires which also migrated to West Africa were Benin, Dahomey, Dogon, Hausa, Igbo- Ukwu, Karem- Bornu, Mali, Mane, Mossi, Nok, Segu, Songhay, Wolof and Yoruba. One of the largest of these kingdoms and empires was the old well - established Ghana Empire, which flourished long before the Akan Tribe arrived and established themselves there sometime between 300 CE and 1235 CE. This great Ghana Empire was situated north of the upper Niger and Senegal valleys, in an area surrounded by countries today known as Guinea, Mali, Senegal and Mauritania. Another big empire, the Kanem- Bornu, stretched from the western banks of the Nile River to the northeast of the Niger River.(3)

On the other hand, scientific studies have shown overwhelming results proving that human beings were living in West Africa as far back as 39,000 BCE. These studies include evidence from carvings, paintings, carbon dating of rocks, etc., and this evidence shows that organized human groups were active by 10,000 BCE in certain areas, such as Achimota and Adwuku in modern Ghana, Yengema in Sierra Leone, Rim in Burkina Faso, and Tiemassas in Senegal.(4)

However, some modern scholars have their own doubts and theories about the history of "Western Sudan", that is today's West Africa. They argue that the only organized civilizations in this region were the later West African civilizations from the third century CE to the tenth century CE. They therefore believe that those empires and kingdoms, such as the ancient Ghana Empire, were founded by migrants from the East to the West, and that most of them had close relationships with Egypt and other civilizations in the Nile Valley. Scientific evidence, including cultural, philosophical and religious artifacts, totems, mummification, circumcision, rituals and other cultural traditions, confirms this westwards migration from the Nile region and Egypt area between the 3rd century CE and the 10th century CE. This migration, it is believed, would have been caused by natural disasters such as drought, floods and pestilence, as well as other catastrophes such as wars, internal family and clan disputes, and refusal to join other ethnic groups' religions or, later on, Islam.(5)

Some of these scientific studies have been able to trace evidence of connections between these migrants from the Nile Valley and some of contemporary cultures among West African ethnic groups. These include the Akan of modern Ghana and the multiple dialects of the Akan language, the Ewe in Ghana and Togo, the Ga in Ghana, and the Igbo and Yoruba of Nigeria, to name just a few groups. For example, some of these cultures share the following aspects of the migrants' belief systems:

1. A belief, first and foremost, in the Creator God, the Supreme Being
2. A belief that the souls of ancestors, the departed, and the unborn are always around with us, the living

Because of these beliefs, some of these migrant ethnic groups, even to this day, begin special meetings and ceremonies with special prayers, first to God the Creator, and then to the other beings. In some cases, these prayers are accompanied by pouring of libation, (small quantities of alcohol or water) onto the ground; these are intended to give thanks to Mother Earth, to ask for God's guidance and help, and to request the support of all the other entities in the ceremony to come. Some of these West African cultures also had various goddesses to help them get their requests through to God, the Supreme Being, for example regarding economic activities.

One example of asking for help through a lesser goddess could be found in the Asante farmers of the Akan tribe. When they visited their farms or went out hunting or fishing, they used to pray to the Earth goddess Asase Yaa, for success in farming and for protection from accidents or attacks by dangerous animals and poisonous reptiles in the bush. The Igbo-speaking people prayed to their most important goddess, Ale or Ala, for help for their various farming activities. The Mossi people prayed to their goddesses for blessings for their farming activities, for their flocks and herds of animals, for enough rainfall to give them abundant crops, and also for good health for all.(6)

Thus, according to the theories of modern scholars, when these numerous migrants moved westwards away from the Nile valley, they turned southwards and settled south of the Sahara Desert, from the Savannah right down to the Guinea Coast. This area has some of the most outstanding physical, climatic and social diversity in the world. Physically, this area has the most extraordinary Sahara Desert to the north, which sends dry, thick dust sometimes as far north as Southern Europe, as well as southwards, right down to the Guinea Coast of the Atlantic Ocean. To the south of this desert is the Savannah, and then the tropical forest region extending as far as the Guinea Coast. The region is full of natural mineral resources, such as gold, diamonds and manganese, and other resources including spices, ivory, timber, and many more. It has especially beautiful tropical vegetation, an extraordinary variety of wild animal and bird species, and rivers and lakes. Because of the region's natural wealth, there were constant migrations into the area.(7)

According to historians of West Africa as well as the oral record, the kingdoms, empires, and ethnic groups that migrated into the "Western Sudan" included the Akan, who went to settle in the already existing Ghana Empire. Then came the empires and kingdoms of Benin, Dahomey, Dogon, Nok, Segu, Songhay, Wolof and Yoruba. The largest of the kingdoms and empires in that region was the Ghana Empire, situated north of the upper Niger and Senegal valleys. The powerful Ghana Empire was surrounded by the kingdoms of Guinea, Mali, Mauritania and Senegal as well as the Kanem-Bornu Empire, which stretched from the western banks of the Nile to north and east of the Niger River. Eventually, some of the ethnic groups which came from the Nile valley to the "Western Sudan" then moved southwards into what is now West Africa; these included the Akan tribe with its numerous groups and dialects, one of the largest of which was the Asante. As well as the Akan, other groups who moved southwards included the Bambara, Bini, Hausa, Mossi, Peul, Seder, Tukulor and Wolof kingdoms.

As already mentioned, this ancient Western Sudan region is today occupied by the following modern nations: Senegal, Gambia, Guinea-Bissau, Guinea, Sierra Leone, Liberia, Côte d'Ivoire, Mali, Burkina Faso, Ghana, Niamey, Benin, Togo, Niger and Nigeria.(8)

Picture 2: Ancient West African Compound

CHAPTER 2

THE MIGRANTS TRY TO ORGANIZE THEMSELVES

a. Cultural Heritage Brought to West Africa

b. Complementary Relationships between Women and Men in West African Societies

c. Motherhood and Reincarnation

a. Cultural Heritage Brought to West Africa

It is believed that the cultural heritage brought by these migrants to their destinations in West Africa included the establishment of Queens, Queen-Mothers, Kings, Chiefs and Sub-Chiefs, as well as family systems. These types of heritage will be described later on in this book. Their heritage also includes economic activities such as weaving and metalwork, artistic activities, and religious systems, including the establishment of priests and priestesses. Another interesting heritage, practiced by only some of these groups, was female circumcision, which will be discussed later in this book(9). These cultural inheritances, and many others, show great evidence of a continued relationship between the migrants from the Nile Valley to West Africa, and the Faros Empires left behind along the Nile and in Egypt.

According to the book, "Tarikh-es-Sudan" (The History Of Sudan), written by the sixteenth-century African historian Abdurrahman Es Sadi, many Egyptian Pharaohs had homes in the Ancient Ghana Empire long before the migration, and this contact continued after the migration. One concrete example of such a relationship was the contact that Egypt's Pharaoh Sneferu, the first of the 4th Dynasty Pharaohs (2613 - 2589 BCE), is believed to have made with the Ghana Empire. Egyptian Pharaohs visited this ancient empire and consulted Priests and Priestesses for guidance and blessings, as they believed in those West African divination systems, which were similar to theirs. This means that the ancient Ghana Empire must actually have existed long before the CE period began.

After all these migrations, West Africa was said to have had very good educational institutions. Some important examples were the universities of Sankore and Songhay in Timbuktu, which were so popular that, it is claimed, students from Asia and Europe came to study there.(10) Trading was also said to be active, and was conducted in West African languages such as Sarakole, a language spoken by the Mande people of Mali, one of the ancient Ghana Empire's ethnic groups. Furthermore, as the historian Abdurrahman Es Sadi wrote in "Tarikh-es-Sudan",(11) there is significant documentary evidence that contact was maintained between the West African migrants and the peoples living in the Nile Valley up to the Mediterranean Sea - for example, through trade.

b. Complementary Relationships between Women and Men in West African Societies

When the various tribes who migrated to West Africa had settled down - before the introduction of Islam by Muslim traders between the 8th and 11th centuries CE or the introduction by Christian Europe of the North Atlantic chattel slave trade in the 15th century CE, followed by colonization and Christianization in the 19th century - women were great cornerstones around which their societies developed.

One Ghanaian author writes: "Obaa na owoo Obarima; Obaa na owoo Ohene". In the Twi dialect of the Akan of modern Ghana, this means, "It's a woman who gave birth to a man; it's a woman who gave birth to a chief". Therefore, as all men came from women's wombs, ancient West African women had great respect from men.[12] [13] There were complementary relationships between women and men in their societies, in which both sacred and secular principles and laws supported this unique interdependency between human females and males. Women were the considered to be the sources of life, full of wisdom which generated inspiration. Thus, according to many reliable ancient written sources and credible oral histories, women in ancient West Africa were highly respected for their expertise, industriousness and creativity, regardless of whether they were from the upper or lower classes, as their contributions were considered essential for the growth and development of their tribes.

The sources I have consulted for this book show that women were considered great loving mothers, creators, state founders, progenitors, warrior defenders, rulers, and consorts; motivating forces in the development and advancement of their nations, as well as great and loving wives. Beside these responsibilities, ancient West African women also took leading roles; complementing their men, in agricultural, architectural and scientific advancement, and the establishment and operation of their societies' educational, cultural, and religious institutions. These women were also effective in leadership roles in business operations, such as manufacturing and commerce, which were conducted in two major languages on a local as well as an international level. The first of these languages was the

Sarakole language, which was spoken by the Soninke tribe of the Ghana Empire; the second, the Mandingo language spoken by the people of Mali.

c. Motherhood and Reincarnation

Because ancient West Africans believed that reincarnation was the basis and meaning of human existence on planet earth, women were greatly respected as the channels for the souls returning to this earth. In most of the tribes (the Akan, Ewe, Ga, Igbo, and Yoruba, to mention just a few), there was a great belief in reincarnation. That is, they believed that the souls of the unborn and of dead ancestors were all with the living, and that women were the channels through which family souls were reincarnated to come and enrich clan existence, as well as to finish their missions on earth.(14) Men, meanwhile, could not bring these souls back to earth physically, but were believed to have contributed spiritually to the reincarnation through their fertilization of the women's eggs.

Because of this great expectation of West African women, these West African tribes believed that women's most important mission on this earth was to learn in many ways and develop great wisdom. Also, they had to celebrate a puberty rite, another learning process, before marrying, having children, breastfeeding them and then, together with their males, bringing them up and educating them until they were old enough to get on with their own lives. However, according to these ancient West African belief systems, these were not the only responsibilities of women. When these children grew up and had their own children and grandchildren, women, as grandmothers and as great-grandmothers, remained cornerstones in many ways for their children, grandchildren and great-grandchildren. Another major responsibility of women was to be good and loving wives who, amongst other things, were able to organize their home's activities. Women took part in all important family decision-making, as well as sharing other major civic responsibilities, so that they stood side by side with their males in their families and their societies in general.

As motherhood was a very important phenomenon in ancient West African societies, it was often a tragedy with great consequences for a woman not to be able to have children. On the other hand, in some societies, those women who could not have children themselves did not find themselves in a very tragic situation. Firstly, families lived very close together. Secondly, some of the tribes had a practice of sending some of the family's young children to live with those women in the extended family who could not have children themselves. Even in modern times, during my anthropological field work in West Africa, I came across this practice. Similarly, ancient oral history suggests, that in some tribes, a man who could not have children (whether through impotency or infertility) did not find life so tragic either. In some ancient tribes of the Savannah, I was told during my anthropological travels, a wife would secretly help in a special way, or a male member of the extended family was asked to offer help.(15)

Motherhood was rewarded in many ways. According to reliable oral history, in some of the tribes such as the Twi speaking people of the Akan tribe, any woman who had had ten children - whether all these children were living or not - was honored in a special grand ceremony, celebrating her great achievement and generous contribution to enriching the clan's existence. This was because population growth in ancient West Africa was seriously affected by diseases and wars.

In some cultures, the achievement of motherhood was rewarded through canonization. The family, the clan and the whole community of a mother who had had many children and contributed to her clan's well-being in other ways, would join together to erect a shrine for her. Other outstanding mothers were immortalized as goddesses for their contributions to the survival and well-being of the human species.(16)

However, views of twins differ greatly across these cultures. In some tribes, for example, in the Akan group and some others, great ceremonies were performed for women who gave birth to twins, as twins were considered to be an omen of good fortune for the mother's tribe. On the other hand, in some of these ancient West African cultures, twins were considered an omen of bad luck for the family, the clan and the community as a whole; these twins would therefore mysteriously die at birth.

Women were also very good at reciting or singing their clans' old stories or poems, or singing other special songs at ceremonies, funerals, or even war fronts. During these ceremonies, "libations" would be performed; that is, Palm Wine, or a local alcoholic drink, or water, would be poured down on Mother Earth. This was to invoke the earth goddess "Asase Yaa", as well as ancestral departed souls or other minor clan gods. Prayers would be recited for their guidance or mediation, according to the purpose of the occasion, so as to seek help from the "Almighty Creator God" or, in the "twi" language of the Akan, the "Oboo Adea Onyankopon".(17) (18)

So women were very good at these ceremonies which were always accompanied by drumming, singing and dancing. Sometimes these ceremonies were held at places dedicated to the worship of these goddesses, who acted as mediators between human beings and the Creator God. Such ceremonial places could be by special rivers, lakes, mountains, rocks, or other spots; some of them were special shrines erected permanently for the worship of these goddesses and ancestors, to ask them for God's help.

As women were afforded great respect in ancient West African cultures, the older a woman became, the more powerful and influential she was, and older women were shown great respect wherever they went. So the men could not possibly make important family, clan or even community decisions without the approval of the oldest women in their families, clans or communities, even though these old women might not have been physically present at the important meetings.

As mentioned earlier, the Akan of both the ancient Ghana Empire and modern Ghana have a saying that stresses the importance of women in their societies. It is: "Obaa na owoo Obarima; Obaa na owoo Ohene", which means, "It's a woman who gave birth to a man; it's a woman who gave birth to a chief".[19] The complementary power that women traditionally had with their men in these ancient cultures was due to the fact that it was recognized that every man has been developed in a woman's womb for some months, and that, after birth, a woman had a great responsibility to take care of a helpless, fragile little human being for a long time. In the same way, in the Christian religion, great importance is also placed on the Virgin Mary, mother of Jesus Christ.

However, as we shall see later on in this work, many civilized cultures in the Western World have deliberately ignored the importance of women's valuable roles in human existence. Their women have been fighting for at least one century for equal, complementary rights between women and men in this modern world, without great success.[20]

Now, to summarize: ancient West African motherhood placed great natural responsibilities on women, which were recognized and accepted in those ancient cultures. Women also had to behave appropriately. Therefore, in most of these cultures, when girls reached puberty, not only did they receive some sort of training in some economic activities, but they also underwent various tribal puberty rites. These ceremonies made them aware of the great responsibilities which lay ahead of them, before they could marry and have children later on.

During these ceremonies, they were taught lessons about good married life with their husbands, how to take good care of their children, and how to take care of and be close to their elderly mothers and fathers, as well as other old family and clan members who might need help until they died. This was in accordance with the popular saying in some West African languages: "First, the parents look after their children; later, the children look after their parents." That is the natural family environment. This responsibility is slowly disappearing in the modern world, especially in Europe. Nowadays, especially in northern European countries, governments have taken over these responsibilities from families. Old people are isolated in very quiet "Old People's Homes" which, however luxurious and comfortable they may be, leave many of the residents feeling lonely. Many of these old people live in comfort, but are depressed and sad. One observer once said to me, "What these old people need to revive them, is to be housed near places where there is energy coming from all those wild actions of "super active" school children running about, shouting, screaming and kicking each other. That is, near schools, children's recreational grounds and other educational institutions, and also near shopping centers". I made no comments, as I, myself, once lived in a "Senior Residence", therefore I was aware of what he was talking about.

However, in most of the ancient West African cultures, whether a woman had had children or not, she received loving care in her old age from her clan. Going through the puberty rite was life insurance in itself, hence the female circumcision ritual during puberty rites, brought from some parts of ancient Egypt, was practiced by only a few of the tribes. Islam also adopted the practice.(21)

Besides motherhood and reincarnation matters, let us now examine the other serious responsibilities of women in their societies in ancient West African cultures, before considering the effects upon these women of Islamization, North Atlantic chattel slave trading, colonialism and the Christian Religion.

CHAPTER 3

ANCIENT WEST AFRICAN WOMEN AS:

a. Queens, Queen-Mothers, Warriors, Great Advisors
b. The Common Women as Great Supporters in Battle
c. Queens, Queen-Mothers and the Common Women as Herbal Medicine Specialists, Spiritual Healers and Priestesses

a. Queens, Queen–Mothers, Warriors, Great Advisors

The matrilineal descent system of heritage in ancient West Africa saw women rule their societies as powerful Queens, side by side with their sons, their sisters' sons, or other close matrilineal royal men as Kings, Paramount Chiefs, or Divisional Chiefs. This is why Western European foreigners called them "Queen-Mothers". This tradition was unlike the traditions of Western cultures in which the Queen could be either the ruler of a kingdom in her own capacity, or a commoner or aristocrat who married a ruling King. In most of those ancient West African cultures, if a woman who should have been a Queen could not take this responsibility due to ill health or other reasons, another woman from the immediate matrilineal royal family, such as her sister, daughter, or sister's daughter, became Queen.

Another important point here is that, in those days, the status and the power of Queens and Queen-Mothers did not always derive from being born or marrying into royal families. Sometimes, such status was achieved, not because women were born into aristocratic families although they were not royal people, nor because they were married to powerful politicians, rich and influential men, or aristocrats. Sometimes there were special reasons for ordinary women to achieve it.

According to some ancient writers and oral history, some Queens and Queen-Mothers derived their status and power from the fact that they were powerful warriors and war leaders, bringing victory for their people, or powerful trade leaders, organizing special trade routes that enabled their societies to prosper through trading. This was simply because such women had wisdom. Therefore, these clever women who raised themselves into these high positions were highly intelligent; they were so clever in many ways that they were also able to preside over judicial cases, without the formal training known in modern times.

These women also exercised control over their societies' domestic matters, giving advice and guidance to the kings, chiefs and sub-chiefs and to the ordinary citizens. This advice could relate to finance, trading, health, education or war, to name some examples. As a matter of fact, some sources claim that ancient West African women were so powerful in their families and clans that, in some cases, men were afraid of their spiritual powers. Some of these men thought that such powers could only have come to these females from the various goddesses they worshipped to help them reach the Almighty God. Some secretly branded some of these super-wise and powerful women witches.

Thus, some Queens and Queen-Mothers were born into royal families but, as explained above, sometimes common women also rose to royal positions, due to their outstanding contribution to their societies.

However, occasionally, some of these Queens were dethroned due to alleged misbehavior. Sometimes, this was because the Queen and her family had not revealed that their ancestors, many generations back, had been slaves, even though it would not have mattered if the family had been honest and open about their origins. On the other hand, in a few cases, a woman who had been, or still was, a slave, became a Queen all the same due to her special and unusual talent.

An example of a common woman who rose to a position of royalty due to her wisdom was Iyoba Idia, a war leader who became the Queen-Mother and whose son, Oba Esigie, became king of Benin. Later on, this Queen-Mother raised an army and went to war to defeat her son's enemies, during the Ida War in the 16th century.[22]

One group of people known for their brave warrior Queens was the Asante Kingdom of the Akan group in West Africa, one of the tribes who migrated southwards from the Ancient Ghana Empire. Some examples included the divisional Queen Edwesohemaa Yaa Asantewaa war against the British Colonialists in 1900. Also Queen - Mothers Ama Seewaa, Kokofuhemaa, Ataa Birago and Yaa Kyaa the Asantehemaa, the Queen - Mother of the Asante Kingdom earlier joined Osei Yaw the Asante King to fight the British army in the city of Kumasi, the capital of the Asante Kingdom, in the 1820s. This war was fought to defend the Asante Kingdom from British colonialism. In one of these wars, a famous war leader Nana Anti Gyan, one of the divisional Chiefs of the Asante Kingdom and Commander of a battalion fighting the British colonialists was captured and beheaded by the British Army on the banks of River Pra in the Asante region.[23]

Other powerful female cavalry fighters were the Fon women of Dahomey. They were such great warriors that their cavalry eventually became a permanent force within their country's army, during the reign of King Ghezo from 1818 to

1858. The Egba Yoruba women's cavalry was also powerful in West Africa in ancient times.

Besides taking part in wars, these West African Queens and Queen-Mothers, due to the power of their matriarchal descent system, could also become great designers and makers of artifacts. They were weavers, architects and builders, besides being clever traders offering financial and commercial advice. Some were also fisher-women, farmers and great educationalists.

Further examples of these powerful Queens and Queen-Mothers were Emose and Orhorho, who were "ogisofs", or rulers, who ruled in succession with their eight brothers after their father's death during the first dynasty of the Benin Empire, 1200 CE. [24]

b. The Common Women as Great Supporters in Battle

Due to the power of the matriarchal descent system, women commoners also played extraordinarily important roles in their societies. Besides being great mothers and wives, they played their parts as great cornerstones in their families, and also as warriors, soldiers, and front-line war supporters in their societies. Some of them actually took arms and fought side by side with their men, whereas some of them, like the Akan women of the ancient Ghana Empire, participated in their wars in different ways. For example, they sometimes presented themselves to sing war songs right at the war front. In the Akan dialect of "twi", they sang "Twe Mmobomme" to give spiritual, physical and moral support to their men, enabling them to withstand the harsh and dangerous battle conditions and crush their enemies.

Before these Akan women took these actions, that is, taking up arms, chanting and dancing, they first poured libations and offered prayers to the Creator God, "Oboo Adee Onyankopon" in the "twi" dialect, asking for help and blessings. They also asked for the support of the lesser goddesses and gods, the spirits of their ancestors, and the newly departed souls of their tribe's women and men, to help the fighters by increasing their spiritual, physical and mental strength, enhancing their ability to fight and win.

c. Queens, Queen-Mothers and the Common Women as Herbal Medicine Specialists, Spiritual Healers and Priestesses

Details of the powerful positions held by West African women in complementarity with their men are, on the whole, beyond the scope of this book. However, to summarize briefly, they were very powerful. As outlined above, Queens, Queen-Mothers, and even some women commoners took their positions, where necessary, as warriors, battle leaders, and front-line Fighters. These women also showed great talents including commerce, industries, education, architecture and handicrafts.

Besides these responsibilities, most of these women - from Queens and Queen-Mothers to common women and the slave women who automatically became respected members of their owners' families - also showed various great talents as herbalists and "medicine women", popularly known as "witch doctors" to the Christian European chattel slave traders. These women were therefore able to contribute also, according to their individual talents, as priestesses and herbalists, offering spiritual healing and other herbal medicine work, and generously providing all kinds of help for the benefit of their people. For example, during battles, they would plead with God the Creator, through their lesser goddesses and gods, to send positive spiritual power and energies to their fighters for them to win; sometimes they would also provide on-the-spot herbal medicine for injured fighters.

On the whole, these women had great belief in the Creator God, "Oboo Adee Onyankopon", but used lesser goddesses and gods as mediators, as well as tools, to reach God. Hence, at the beginning of healing performances and other important and serious activities or meetings, libation prayers were performed and a drink was poured down on Mother Earth or "Asaase Yaa" for the Creator God. At the end of the libations, it was always said that such and such would happen if it was the "Will of God", or "Se Onyame Pe a" in the "twi" dialect.[25]

CHAPTER 4

THE INTRODUCTION OF ISLAM TO NORTHERN PART OF ANCIENT WEST AFRICA

The British historian and traveler J. S. Spencer Trimingham observed that, in ancient West Africa before the introduction of Islam and Christianity, the most important phenomenon was that religion and society were so bound up that it was impossible to separate the two. The West Africans believed in a Supreme Being, the Creator God of the whole universe:

> "Africans believe in a Supreme Being who created the whole cosmos. It is regarded, though not necessarily worshiped, as Creator and ultimate source of all life, but in contrast to the created worlds of Spirits. It is impersonal, unknowable, and communion with It is impossible. The Creator is the generator of spirit force which, after animating the various forms of creation return to the Creator. The world is created in harmony. The forms of creation temporary receptacles of divine force, radiate it, and the interaction of radiations may disturb the harmony of the divine cosmos. The purpose of the all-embracing ritual of village life is to maintain or restore the harmony. This basic conception of power pervading the universe, possessed by ancestors, men, animals and things, makes the world a sphere of dynamic relationship between forces. Religion is primarily ritual, the action of man to maintain power in equilibrium and preserve. The harmony of this dynamic cosmos... Man never dies because life force is eternal."(26)

This is how this British Christian visitor interpreted West African religions in which The Creator God was already known. Therefore, before the introduction of Islam into both regions of Western Sudan - that is, the North of the Sahara Desert area as well as Southern Sahara - Trimingham also observed that:

> "Religion and society are one. Each social group functions as a religious community. So bound up together are religion and society that neither can be understood in isolation. The Muslim traders who arrived at the northern part of West Africa between the 9th and the 11th centuries brought with them their religion, therefore, this is how Islam began its penetration, so that in a slow process, "monotheism" was introduced to the areas where they started their trading."(27)

This shows that the West Africans believed in a Supreme Being, who created the whole cosmos. This Creator also created spirit forces, including the living, the dead and nature, so that each of these has its own function but also works in harmony with the others. For example, when a living person died, the incident was considered a matter of making changes. Therefore, as society and religion were considered to be one, the old women in the families were the harmonizers and restorers. As they were the heads of their families, who were supported by the old male family members, these old women were greatly respected.(28)

Therefore, with the introduction of Islam and its patriarchal descent system in which males ruled, those West African women who lived in the areas where Muslims settled lost their prestigious status in their communities. One major change in the lives of the women when they embraced the religion of Islam was the fact that,

> "Women, regarded as being in a constant state of ritual impurity, are not allowed to enter mosques... They are ignorant and may be unclean."[29]

Also, after a West African woman who had converted to Islam had given birth, she was considered impure and was not allowed to take part in prayers until forty days after delivery. Later on, when Muslim formal education was introduced, both boys and girls were sent to school at the age of 6, but Muslim girls were withdrawn by the age of 10.[30]

Even though both Christianity and Islam have their roots in Judaism religion, which observes a matriarchal descent system where the mother is a great cornerstone for the family, both Muslim and Christian missionaries in West Africa ignored mothers' positions in their teachings. Regarding the Christian missionaries, the role of the "Virgin Mary", the famous Mother of Jesus Christ who is important in Christianity, was completely ignored.

However, some observers argue that the missionaries' neglect of West African women's positions and roles in society was due to the fact that these missionaries' own cultures - both Arab Muslims and European Christians - were based on patriarchal descent systems and patriarchal power structures. This system was then introduced into their religions back home. Therefore, these foreigners were afraid of the power of the West African women; they were not used to the phenomenon, and so suppressed these women.

On the other hand, in those days before Islam was introduced to those regions, women not only held domestic and reproductive roles - as wives, mothers, sisters, grandmothers, daughters, aunts, and so on - but also a few women rose in their societies to become elite in some ways. One example of an elite woman who rose to hold a high position in her society and to perform very special rituals was Enheduanna. She was a priestess and consort of the Moon God, Nanna, in Mesopotamia around 2300 BCE. Elite women were patrons of architecture or musicians, and some royal women served as regents and had political influence on their husbands and sons. However, not much is known about the common women as they remained in the background of their societies.

Consequently, the traditional great barrier between men and women caused by the patriarchal descent system ultimately influenced every aspect of life in ancient Mesopotamian society, and this continued until the emergence of Islam in the Arabian Peninsula in the year 622 CE. This religion, together with Christianity and Judaism, sprang from the teachings of the patriarchal Prophet Abraham. This tradition of male superiority in these foreign religions was then transferred to West Africa, destroying the West African matriarchal descent system in most of those societies forever.(31)

The arrival of Muslim traders caused much confusion in West African societies, with their merchandise and their Islamic teachings from the Holy Koran. First, in the northern region of the Sahara Desert where Muslims started to trade and establish Islam from the 9th to the 11th century, women's traditional roles in their families, clans, societies and their own religions and social structures completely collapsed.

Second, as a result, there arose a mixture of traditions and new religious practices. This further confused the people in the region so that the Muslim system of patriarchal descent was imposed in all spheres of life; first, in the northern part of the Sahara Desert, and then southwards, into West Sudan.

Third, suddenly, the old, extended family structures gave way to a simple matrimonial family, consisting of a man, his wife or wives, his slaves and his children. This new family system brought about further complications.

For example, in the powerful matriarchal family system, members of some of extended families would own lots of plots of land together, with the deliberate intention of binding the families together. Sometimes dozens and dozens and dozens of extended family members could have joint ownership of the same piece of land together; this bound families together, so that members offered moral and financial support as well as solidarity whenever any member or members needed help.[32]

Trimingham therefore concludes that:

> "The allegiance of individuals to Islam and disownment of the family cult may weaken natural ties and lead to the formation of new ones outside the family."[33]

> "The increasing spread of Islamic cultural influences and practices to the native commoner populations in the eleventh century resulted in more widespread practice of polygamy within the patriarchal Islamic social structure... Bride price too, must be understood within the context of the ancient African matrilineal societies where women held valued and privileged positions, rather than reflecting patriarchal notions of a commodity exchange at marriage."

Therefore, in those days in ancient West African marriage systems, the bride price paid to the woman's family "was viewed as a guarantee that the betrothed woman would be respected, honored, and protected."[34]

CHAPTER 5

MIGRATION FURTHER SOUTH OUT OF CONFUSION

The confusion brought about by the introduction of Islam in the northern part of West Africa, and then in the Western Sudan, became a major reason for the southwards migration of many societies. For example, the Akan from the ancient Gana (Ghana) Empire in Western Sudan, which had many dialects and included the Asante group of people, migrated southwards from the southern Savannah area, towards the Guinea Coast of the Atlantic Ocean. Eventually, part of this coastal region of the Guinea Coast where some of these migrants settled, including the Akan, was named the Gold Coast by English chattel slave traders, because of the abundance of gold deposits in the region's geological makeup. Later on this region became known as Ghana. During the migration, some of the Akan groups even went westwards to what is known today as Ivory Coast.

This Akan tribe and many others refused to accept Islam. By doing so, the Akan tribe was one of the migrant groups that preserved its matriarchal descent system, as well as the strong bond between religion, customs and social and economic life in general. All these operated together in those days. In other parts of black West Africa south of the Sahara Desert, the arrival of Islam brought about changes, some positive for some of the groups there, but some with very negative effects on the lives of the tribes' members.

One example of the positive effects for certain groups was that the men in the tribes which accepted the culture of polygamy brought by the Muslims abandoned their complementary existence with women with great pleasure. However, the negative influence was far more devastation for their women. Women lost their natural position as cornerstones, war leaders, warriors, great traders, top-class medicine women, advisors, educators, etc. All the women's expertise and positions in those newly-established Muslim societies disappeared, so that women gradually came to be viewed as sex objects who were considered only fit to control the kitchen and household affairs.[35] Eventually, the importance of extended family contact culture also disappeared for ever.

Other black West African tribes south of the Sahara Desert who resisted the influence of Islam were the Gurmanshe and the two Mossi kingdoms: the Wagadugu, which was founded about 1050 CE, and the Yatenga, also founded about 1170 CE. Since then, these tribes have been occupying the north of the River Volta in an area now known as Burkina Faso, bordering the north side of the present day Ghana. They also resisted the influence of Islam for some time.[36]

On the other hand, some of the West African tribes, for example some of the Bambara people of Mali who adopted a name meaning "a separation from mother", broke off from the matriarchal descent system to adopt the Muslim patriarchal descent system. Meanwhile, other groups of the Bambara people who called themselves "mother-child", together with many West African tribes like the Serer and the Peul, held on to their matriarchal descent systems for a long time, like the Akan.

Therefore, women's power started to erode in both the north and south regions of West Africa, as in the families who adopted Islam, children had to take their fathers' last names instead of traditional ancestral names to preserve their history. For example, in this new system, five brothers and sisters would have the same surname.

Eventually, when males started to rule large city-states in the Islamic-dominated region of West Africa, they used the principles of Islam to support, maintain and rationalize their power (37; 38). Islam remained limited to the northern part and the Sahara Desert region for some time, until it was seriously introduced to the southern part of the Sahara Desert, when the Christian Europeans were finishing their chattel slave trading on the Guinea Coast, and introducing their colonialism and their Christian religion.

During this period, there was a kind of competition for converts between Islam and Christianity, at a time when West Africans on the Guinea Coast were demoralized and confused by the damaging activities of the representatives of God's two great Prophets, Jesus Christ and Mohamed. The same representatives who had been selling them as "things", as "commodities", as "animals", now introduced those left behind to God for Its salvation, by converting them.

Eventually, the Muslims started to move a little southwards towards the Guinea Coast. This was the period in which the Christian European chattel slave traders, who arrived in the 15th century CE, traded first in gold and spices, then later mainly in the "human commodity" were preparing their scrambling for colonies, and then at the same time introducing their Christianity as salvation for the confused "heathens".

However, in this study, as already mentioned, I am not dealing with the activities of the Muslim traders who were the first to arrive from the Middle East to the northern part of West Africa, who traded in goods such as salt, and artifacts as well as buying of local slaves, while at the same time also converting the people they met there to embrace Islam. Detailed description of the slave-trading activities of Arab Muslims and their introduction of their religion are, as already mentioned, beyond the scope of this book. Rather, in the following chapters, I am concentrating on those tribes, especially the Akan, one of those ethnic groups who moved slowly from the ancient Ghana Empire, then to the Guinea Coast, to resist Islam and its patriarchal descent family system, a system which was being introduced by the Muslim Traders in the Northern Sudan, that is, Northern part of West Africa.

Another important reason why I am going to concentrate on the Akan ethnic group with its numerous dialects, apart from the fact that they resisted the religion of Islam, is that when they moved southwards they also had to fight the Christian British chattel slave traders who had just finished their lucrative trading in black humans, and were trying to colonize and Christianize the various confused tribes along the Guinea Coast.

Ironically, this Akan ethnic group migrated southwards in order to hold fast to their matriarchal descent system which was tightly bound to their culture and religion. But then, unfortunately, they were completely overwhelmed by the great tragedy they also suffered when they got to the Guinea Coast, which was caused by the effect of the chattel slave trading that was conducted by the Christian Europeans who arrived on the Guinea Coast in the 15th century CE, and lasted for nearly 400 years.

Let us see now how chattel slavery trading, or the trading in humans as if they were "commodities", or "things", or "animals" in that part of the Guinea Coast which became the Gold Coast, and now Ghana, was introduced, and how it affected the women there in particular. Besides, as already mentioned, this tragedy was then immediately followed by colonization and Christianization by the same Christians who had just been trading in human commodities. How did West African women bear the brunt of this extraordinary tragedy? What then also happened to the Akan people who were left behind on the Coast and tried to resist colonization and Christianization by the same Christian European chattel slave traders?

PART 2

CHAPTER 6

CHRISTIAN EUROPE INITIATES THE GUINEA COAST-NORTH ATLANTIC CHATTEL SLAVE TRADING

Chattel slave trading was initiated by Christian European traders on the Guinea Coast from the 15th century CE. This was long before they started to colonize and Christianize the natives of this region in the 19th century, although they brought their own Christian pastors to bless their lucrative business from the 15th century. As mentioned above, the tragedy of Christian European chattel slave trading, from the Guinea Coast across the North Atlantic Ocean to the Americas and to the Caribbean, left deep scars on human memory that can never be removed.

In this chapter, I deal briefly with chattel slave trading from the Guinea Coast across the North Atlantic Ocean to the Americas and the Caribbean. This history, which lasted for nearly 400 years, could otherwise occupy volumes of books. This is because my main aim in writing this book is to give an overview of the causes of some of the everlasting damaging effects upon West African women of these strange and hard-to-believe phenomena.

Christian Portuguese chattel slave traders first initiated this trade on the Guinea Coast from 1470, and then were joined by most of the empires and kingdoms of Christian Europe. By 1482, these Portuguese traders had built permanent trading forts at a few places along the Guinea Coast. They were then followed by other Christian European countries, as we shall see later on.

The damages done by this type of slavery to West African matriarchal descent systems, as well as to women's complementary existence with their men on the Guinea Coast, have so far been irreparable.

In the past, some scholars argued that the success of this tragic trading was partly due to the fact that these foreigners, whether through deliberate planning or not, introduced more and more types of powerful European weapons, encouraging these natives to fight among themselves and produce more of the "human commodity". Also, the widespread sale of strong European alcoholic drinks ultimately made the natives completely dependent on the Christian traders. The argument continues that, after achieving their goal of dependency, these Christian traders sometimes refused to accept gold as part-payment for their weapons and their strong alcoholic drinks. Instead, they demanded only human beings as payment for their above-mentioned goods. For example, at times the payment for one bottle of strong European alcoholic drink was one able human being. Of course, this situation triggered more battles and raids amongst the "trapped" natives on the Guinea Coast, upsetting their normal way of life. In the end, women and children became the greatest victims.

The phenomenon of slavery in general, which was the misuse of a human being by a fellow human being as moveable or immoveable property has, for whatever reason, been part of human existence on this planet stretching back to ancient civilizations. Therefore, slavery as an institution existed all over the world as the primitive life of humans started to develop into life in settlements in ancient times. Since then, slavery has been a natural weakness of humanity. However, the chattel slave trading in West Africa on the Guinea Coast was unique. In the end, it formed the basis of the Western Industrial Revolution and the excessive material wealth of Christian Europe.

This also resulted in the introduction of Christianity in West Africa's coastal regions by these same civilized Christian European chattel slave traders, towards the end of their business activities buying and selling human beings. Therefore, their colonization and Christianization tactics were played side by side, resulting in a scramble for West African colonies by many Western European countries, especially by the British and the French.(39) Finally, in today's modern world, the globalization of Western materialism has also affected these regions badly.

It is also interesting to note that the development of civilization in ancient Near East empires - such as Greece, Rome, Mesopotamia and Israel, and even, in much earlier times, ancient monarchies such as Egypt and Nubia (modern Sudan, which is even older than Egypt) - were also based on slavery, but not on chattel slavery. Slaves in earlier and ancient times remained in the same environment as their masters and, in the case of Egypt, even worked close by their masters. In ancient Europe, some slaves could buy their freedom; and, as mentioned above, in ancient West Africa some slave women even rose to become queens and queen mothers. This was unfortunately not the case in the West African chattel slavery introduced by the Christian European traders, who shipped their slaves away from Africa, thousands of miles away across the North Atlantic Ocean. However, what happened to these chattel slaves who were shipped like "things" to the Americas and Caribbean, the brutal and inhuman way that these "things" were shipped and then treated at their destinations, is beyond the scope of this work.(40)

Eventually, as Christian European trading of gold, spices and human beings became more and more concentrated on chattel slaves, the socio-political and socio-economic systems along the Guinean Coast changed. Strong kingdoms became

stronger and more powerful, while others b
and more helpless. People became mor
dependent on the Christian European's powe
and strong alcoholic drinks, the supply of
depended on the production of slaves to pa
commodities. This vicious circle made the entire s ... so
complicated that more conflicts and battles were triggered amongst the natives on the Guinea Coast.

Finally, the whole phenomenon became a vicious circle. The tragic result was that the normal economic activities of Africans along the West African coast collapsed, from farming, fishing, hunting, metal works, weaving, and pottery making to trading with the Arabs and, before that, with the Carthaginians and Phoenicians who used to sail along the Guinea Coast to carry out "silent trading". More energy was put into supplying the human commodity to Christian European chattel slave traders, who even came with their own pastors and their Holy Bibles to bless their buying activities.(41)

Paradoxically, Christianity and chattel slave trading originated from the same source; the guns to produce slaves and the Christian Holy Bible were both brought by the same Christians from their civilized European Christian nations. Once, when I was traveling around Ghana undertaking anthropological field work, an old retired school teacher I met said to me:

> "You know something, we, who were supposed to be "Primitive" did not ship our people to Europe for the "Civilized Christian Europeans" to buy. These civilized European Christians came all the way here to us in West Africa, to us they termed, "primitive ignorant heathens", who were supposed not to know anything about God, The Creator. They came to confuse us on purpose, by giving us their strong alcoholic drinks and guns, to enable

us to produce more and more of this "human commodity" for them to sell to enrich their nations. And then, after they had achieved their aim, that is, after they had achieved solid economic basis for their civilization and their industrial development, they made changes. That is, we, they termed "Heathens", as if we had no idea about God, The Creator, became helpless, demoralized and confused. It was then at this period in our history that these same Christians "abolished" the sale of humans as commodities and then colonized us at the same time that they introduced us, who, they claimed had no idea about The Creator God, to their Christian Holy Bible."

This old man, who had been head teacher of a European Christian missionary school, surprised me with his harsh words, but I did not want to comment. In the beginning I said to myself that he must have known what he was talking about, as he worked with European Christian missionaries in schools for many years. Then, at last, I gathered courage and asked him whether he was a Christian himself, as even though he worked with these Christians, he might not have been a member of their church. He answered, "Yes, of course, I am. If you cannot beat them, you join them".

The following chapter is just a brief account of how the White Christian Europeans conducted their chattel slave trading activities from the 15th century CE. That is, a tale of how humans were traded as if they were "commodities", or "things", in that part of the Guinea Coast of West Africa which became the Gold Coast, and now Ghana, and how women's heritage was completely destroyed forever.

Picture 3: Chattel Slaves Being Marched From Inland To The Coast

CHAPTER 7

A BRIEF ACCOUNT OF THE CHRISTIAN EUROPE'S CHATTEL SLAVE TRADING ON THE GUINEA COAST (GOLD COAST, NOW GHANA)

This chapter will be just a brief account of the Christian European chattel slave trading in that part of the Guinea Coast which later became Gold Coast, and is now Ghana. This dark period in the Guinea Coast's history was followed by colonization and Christianization. These three phenomena destroyed forever West African Akan women's social position as cornerstones for their families, their clans and their societies as a whole.

The Guinea Coast women were toppled by the new order brought by the European Christian chattel slave traders, coming from their own patriarchal descent family systems, which was also introduced through their Christian religion and colonization activities. Some observers have argued that the new religion, Christianity, was not the problem, as even the Virgin Mary, mother of the great prophet Jesus Christ, was the greatest cornerstone in this physical world for her son.

The services of those Akan women who were sold as chattel slaves, together with other West African chattel slaves, were used as foundation cornerstones for the Christian West's Industrial Revolution and the resulting material wealth in the Western World, which was mainly based on these slave's labor in the Americas and Caribbean.

As already stated above, a full account of the European Christian's chattel slave trade on the Guinea Coast - which lasted for nearly 400 years, from the 15th century to sometime in the 19th century - is beyond the scope of this chapter.

The European Christians started their economic activities by buying slaves from the Guinea Coast, not for their own use back home in Europe, but as commodities to be shipped to the Americas and Caribbean. There they carried out New World economic activities including the production of cotton, sugar, rice, molasses and wool, and the mining of silver and other precious metals.

Many Christian European kingdoms were actively involved in the slave trade, including Portugal, Spain, France, England (subsequently Great Britain), Prussia (Brandenburgers), Netherlands, the Danish-Norwegian Kingdom, and Sweden. However, before Christian European traders arrived on the Guinea Coast, Phoenicians and Carthaginians from the Eastern Mediterranean region had already been trading with West Africans peacefully, in what was known as "The Silent Trade".

These foreign traders arrived in ships, which they anchored in the Atlantic Ocean along the Guinea Coast. They came to the beaches to leave their beautiful beads and other artifacts on the sand, away from the high tide, and then ran away very quickly back onto their ships, as they did not think it was safe to meet these jet-black human beings. Next, the jet-black Africans brought lots of gold dust and nuggets to where the beads were and, taking the beads, left the gold as payment and ran off very quickly to hide in the bushes. Then the strangers came out of their ships again, quickly taking the gold away as payment for their goods.

This strange but interesting trade continued for years. To this day these beads, known locally as "Aggrey Beads", are sometimes found in the sand along the Guinea Coast of Ghana.(42)

Later on, Christian Europeans were introduced to West Africa's Guinea Coast by Christopher Columbus's success. He was originally born in Genoa in Italy, but went to Portugal as a young man to seek employment. He and his fellow Portuguese sailors reached the shores of the Guinea Coast, anchored their ship and went to the beach in the 15th century CE, a few years before 1471. There were other Portuguese sailors who were already collecting slaves from the West African coast and the small islands offshore; however, it was Christopher Columbus and his team who first reached the part of the Guinea Coast which became known as the Gold Coast, and later Ghana.

Therefore, the historical records suggest that Portugal first initiated the Guinea Coast chattel slave trading, many centuries after Arab traders had brought Islam to the northern region of West Africa between the 9th and 11th Centuries CE.

In this period, Christian Portugal had started to develop its agricultural and other economic activities under the dynasty that had been founded by the Grand Master of the Christian Religious Military Order of Avis, after the Muslim Arab colonialists had been driven from the Iberian Peninsula, especially Spain. Therefore, workers were being recruited from outside Portugal, especially from Milan and Genoa in Italy, to come and work there and build up the economy.

Therefore, from the beginning of 1400, Portuguese sea farers started sailing down through the small coastal islands off the coast of West Africa looking for gold and workers. In 1441, two Portuguese sea captains, called Antao Goncalves and Nuno Tristao, sailed their ship southwards from Portugal towards the West African coast. When they got to Cabo

Branco, now Mauritania, they managed to capture twelve Africans, put them on their ship and bring them back to Portugal, where they sold them as "chattel slaves", as "commodities", as "things". From then on, Christian Portugal's Christian chattel slave traders raided villages, capturing men, women and children from the islands off the West African Coast, including Cape Verde, Fernando Po (now Bioko) and Sao Tome.

In 1442, the first shipload carrying chattel slaves and gold from these islands landed in Portugal. In 1444, a Portuguese company was established in Lagos, Portugal; it sent its first ship to West Africa, which returned with 235 kidnapped African chattel slaves. As a result of this successful enterprise, Pope Nicholas V issued "Romanus Pontifex", a "Papal Bull" which granted the Portuguese perpetual monopoly of gold and chattel slave trading with Africa.

In 1471, a young sailor from Genoa called Christopher Columbus came to Portugal to look for employment. He joined other sailors and, with his co-captain, they sailed along the West African Coast. After days of sailing, they anchored their ship on the coast, came ashore and entered a little village. To their amazement they saw that all the rivers entering the sea there were full of gold nuggets. On meeting the village chief they saw that he, like all the villagers, was stark naked, and that he had heavy gold nuggets hanging down from his locked hair. The impressed Columbus, and his colleagues named this village "Al Mina" (The Mine); today, the town is known as "El Mina or Edina", in the west coast of Ghana.(43)

The next move of these sailors was to capture as many of these jet-black beings as possible; they were not sure whether these "beings" were proper human beings, with souls like white Christian Portuguese people, and therefore thought they could be sold. These captive Africans had no idea where they were being taken. At last, when these people landed in Portugal, their interaction with their masters showed that these slaves were tough human beings with souls, just like those who had been captured before them in the West African coastal islands.

Chattel Slavery on the Guinea Coast Gathers Momentum

The great success of Christopher Columbus and his team opened the gateway for other Christian European kingdoms to start "commodity" trading along the Guinea Coast. At first, the Christian European traders arrived in the Guinea Coast to buy spices, gold and slaves, also known in those days as "Black Gold". Later on, their commercial activities were concentrated only on buying the human commodity, the "Black Gold"; in return, they sold the Africans firearms, including flint guns and gunpowder, and various strong alcoholic drinks, including rum and the famous Scandinavian Aquavit.

From the Guinea Coast, these Christian traders sailed ships overloaded with chattel slaves to the Caribbean and the Americas. There, they sold their "goods" to European settlers, who were busy with their sugar plantations, rice fields, cotton farms and silver and copper mines. In return, these traders bought sugar, molasses and other goods, and sailed directly to Europe to sell their goods. Then these traders sailed back to the Guinea Coast with strong alcoholic drinks and weapons. Hence, this trading phenomenon became known as: "Triangle Trading".(44)

Building of Forts and Slave Trading Posts

While this trading on the Guinea Coast was progressing, the Christian Europeans acquired pieces of land from the local tribal chiefs along the West African Atlantic Guinea Coast; built themselves forts and castles, as well as smaller trading posts along the coast. This enabled them to carry on their trading safely and successfully, as European merchant ships anchored off-shore at these castles, forts and posts. Then the local African fishermen rowed their small fishing boats to the merchant ships and, loading them with European merchandise, and rowed ashore to deliver their goods to the Castles and Forts. They then rowed back to the merchant ships, their boats packed with slaves from the dungeons of these castles, forts and posts.

All the Christian European countries engaged in this "Black Gold" trading had their own trading residences. These castles, forts and small posts built along that part of the Guinea Coast that became the Gold Coast and now Ghana are listed in chapter 15 of this book. In these forts and castles lived the trading companies' managing directors, with their staff and their Christian pastors, who prayed to God through Jesus Christ for His blessings on their activities.

In these establishments there also lived other staff members who also came from various European countries to work. For example, the traders brought their own medical doctors, who were in charge of the traders' health, and also saw to it that only healthy slaves were shipped. These traders also brought their own European smiths, to make heavy metal chains to put around the slaves' hands and ankles. There were soldiers in the various European forts, who protected their establishments from the aggression of other Europeans, and sometimes also from the attacks of the natives, who on many occasions came from the interior to attack these white Christian traders in their castles and forts. Two such native attacks were organized by the Asante King, Nana Opoku Ware (Oware), and also by a man called Asemani, from the kingdom of Akwamu.(45)

The soldiers also kept order among their own fellow countrymen, who sometimes had serious psychological problems. However, one of their most important tasks of these soldiers was to maintain order amongst the slaves who were kept in dungeons of the castles and forts, as fights and commotion often occurred among these slaves waiting to be shipped. Some of these slaves fought each other; some bit each other's noses, ears and faces; some were trodden upon; some children and women were mishandled sexually, as well as in various dangerous ways. Some soldiers also worked on the ships, organizing the loading of the slave-cargo.

Despite all the different precautions taken in these forts, thousands of European Christian traders died from diseases such as malaria, dysentery, syphilis and tapeworms. But in short, what went on between the traders themselves in these forts every day was beyond human comprehension: rape, theft, mutiny, prostitution, gluttony, fist fighting, homesickness and alcoholism. The commotion in these forts was so bad that, in some instances, some of the drunken Christian traders could not even remember their own names or where they came from. The details of what happened within these European forts are, however, beyond the scope of this book.(46)

How Did Christian Europeans Acquire Their Chattel "Commodity"?

Eventually, the nature of this chattel "commodity" trading on the coast changed. As mentioned above, the Christian Europeans placed more emphasis on the human commodity rather than other goods, and therefore refused to accept gold for their merchandise anymore. In the end, the African slave suppliers had to accept one bottle of some kind of a strong alcoholic drink from Europe, in exchange for one able human being. However, when these Christians run out of alcohol, and while they waited for their ships from Europe to bring fresh supplies, then they would accept gold for the time being.

Eventually the African slave suppliers from inland, as well as their various tribal collaborators living along the coast, became highly addicted to European alcoholic drinks. They then had to buy more weapons, in order to enable them to fight amongst themselves, to capture more war prisoners and exchange them for strong European alcoholic drinks.

Picture 4: The March From Inland To The Coast Continues

CHAPTER 8

CAPTURED WOMEN AND CHILDREN AS "COMMODITIES"

a. From the Interior to the Coast

b. The Slave Market

c. The Shipment of Female and Male Chattel Slave Cargo

a. From the Interior to the Coast

During this period of foreign slavery on the West African Coast, women were captured either as a result of war, or through some kind of conflict, or as payment of a debt. This was unlike the usual practice before the arrival of white traders, where slaves became their captors' kin, living with or near their masters to carry out various services. This old order changed; in the new order, slaves were sent far away to other continents, sold like "commodities", and had no kin. The women slaves were bound in chains like the male slaves, and those coming from regions far inland had to walk for several days to reach the forts and castles on the coast, where they would be sold.

Some of these women had children with them, or had babies hanging on to their empty breasts. The young children walked alongside their mothers. Sometimes these women, babies and children would fall sick, and if whipping by the native traders escorting them to the coast did not make them walk properly, they were left behind in the bush to die, or to be eaten alive by wild animals. Some also died from poisonous snake-bites, or from heavy falling trees and branches during tropical rainfalls, storms and lightning.

Eventually, after many days walking through the jungles, deep rivers with no bridges, and tropical thunderstorms, with iron chains around them and food carried on their heads, the surviving male and female slaves would reach the coast and be sent to the dungeons underneath the Christian European buyers' castles and forts.

The next step was that these foreign Christian dealers and their teams in the various castles and forts, including their medical doctors, would inspect the "merchandise". If satisfied, the foreign traders would pay for the "goods" with weapons and bottles of strong European alcoholic drinks. All this time, the slave mothers would still have their babies and young children hanging on to them in these dark, dirty, wet dungeons, with no windows and no fresh air, full of fellow slaves - men and children, young and old - with temperatures of over 30° Celsius.

In these dungeons, some of these slaves would be vomiting, urinating, defecating, weeping, and shouting. Some would also be helping others by biting off their ears, noses or lips, to make them unfit for sale. Some of them died, including children, women and their babies, who did not have enough of their mothers' milk or other food, or enough fresh air. In these dungeons, each of which had a capacity of several hundred, slaves would be given just enough food to keep them alive and strong enough for sale on market day.

In the meantime, some of the women were kept especially to be housemaids or to fulfil the sexual desires of some of the establishments' men, as the forts had only male occupants. There were exceptional instances where a Christian European pastor brought his wife, or a Governor brought his sister or wife to the Coast; but this was only for a short period at a time, as life expectancy was very short. Many traders died within one year of their arrival, so it was a great risk for European women to come and live there. Among the most deadly diseases were all kinds of fevers, including malaria, but the Danish-Norwegian traders simply called all these fevers "Klimatfeber".[47]

Eventually, some of the Christian European kingdoms allowed their citizens in the slave trade industry on the Guinea Coast to keep local women as wives, girlfriends or slaves, for three reasons. First, this would satisfy their sexual desires, reducing the negative effects of their loneliness. Second, marrying women from the local communities would help to create alliances with local warlords, ensuring their much-needed help in producing more human commodities. Third, mulatto boys from these relationships could fulfil the roles of soldiers, security men, and workers inside the forts, even from the age of ten.

However, there were a few mulatto boys who were very fortunate to be sent out of the Guinea Coast to Europe to have good education. One example was Frederic Petersen (1710-1789). His father was a Danish soldier at the Danish-Norwegian slave traders' residence, Christiansborg Castle, at Osu, a suburb of Accra, which became the capital town of the Gold Coast. Frederic's father died when he was a child, and at the age of ten he enlisted as a soldier at the castle. He was later adopted by a Danish pastor called Pastor Svane; he was sent to Denmark, where he had a very good education up to university level, and changed his name to "Fredericus Petri Svane Africanus". He studied at Copenhagen University in Denmark, and became a theologian, even though he had problems with his examiners at the last moment. He left Denmark to return to the Guinea Coast as a missionary. There life failed him and, after his imprisonment there, he returned to Denmark. Again, he went through so many great difficulties and miseries that, unfortunately, his life ended in the most unusual tragedy. He died a beggar in Denmark.(48)

As for the mulatto girls connected to the slave-traders' castles, forts and trading posts, most of them became prostitutes, serving the Christian men in the forts as well as the visiting merchant traders. A few of these young mulatto girls also became wives, entering very short-lived marriages at an early age.

The slave mothers and their misused mulatto children remained slaves, who could be disposed of at any time. Most mulatto slave children therefore received no formal education. On the whole, these conditions created still more suffering for West African women and their young daughters who were publicly raped even in the dungeons, as well as serving as "call girls" for the men in these Christian establishments, while they waited to be shipped.

b. The Slave Market

On the day when these human commodities were sold, merchant ships from Christian Europe would already be anchored outside the particular castle or fort holding a slave market. Before the market was officially opened, the resident's medical doctor would inspect the women to be sold that day, assessing whether their sexual organs were normal and without any problem; whether they had firm breasts, indicating that they were not very old; whether they had healthy teeth; whether they could hear well, walk properly and see clearly. The babies hanging on to their mothers' empty breasts, as well as the young toddlers following them, had no value, and were therefore ignored in these medical examinations.

Next, the forts' soldiers would shave these naked women, the girls, and also the men. The hairs from their heads and under-arms, their eyelashes, their eyebrows and their pubic hairs would all be shaven off. Then palm oil would be smeared onto their naked bodies, so that the foreign buyers would not be able tell which were too old and therefore unfit to buy. After these preparations, the slaves would be sent to the market place, all naked, for sale in the castle or fort's courtyard; all these slaves would be in iron chains in the hot sun. These preparations would be followed by the Christian pastors' prayers, appealing to the Almighty God, in the name of Jesus Christ, for His Blessings for successful negotiations with the overseas traders who had been rowed ashore in small boats hired from local fishermen. These Christian European businessmen could be English (or British from the 18th Century), or they could be French, Dutch, Spanish, Prussian, Swedish, Portuguese, Italian, or from the Danish-Norwegian Kingdom.

c. The Shipment of Female and Male Chattel Slave Cargo

At last, when the sales were over, after the merchants had made their choices and expressed their satisfaction, the purchased slaves had to be marked with the various companies' trading logos. The smiths of the castle or fort would mark these commodities. A fire would be lit, and the metal logo of a company would be put in the glowing hot fire to become red-hot, before being removed from the fire. Then the naked skin of both the females' and the males' upper chest would be smeared with palm oil, and then the glowing hot iron logo would be pressed onto the skin, sparking particles of hot oil around. However, as the area was particularly sensitive for the females because of their breasts, many of these women and girls developed dangerous sores on their breasts. Consequently, these markings were eventually made on the females' backs.

When the transactions were over and the slaves marked, then the white soldiers, with their whips, would march the slaves, women, men and children, still in metal chains, to the beaches just outside the residences. Some of these women, crying, were followed by their unmarked young children or had their unmarked babies still hanging onto their empty, painful breasts. The children would be screaming, crying and sobbing, and were covered with flies and mosquitoes, even during the day time. They were all naked like their mothers and the male slaves.

At the beach, the tall and muscular local fishermen would be waiting, hired to pack these "goods" onto their boats and row them to the merchant ships, which were anchored about one to two hundred meters away in the Atlantic Ocean. However, as a final blow to the slave-mothers, the Christian European soldiers would snatch the babies and children, who had been holding fast to their mothers, and throw them onto the beaches. There the hungry and aggressive hyenas, which had been pacing up and down the beaches looking for food, would come and eat them.

Then, as the muscular local fishermen, who would be under the influence of those strong European alcoholic drinks, started rowing towards the huge European slave ships, these confused and frightened women, howling and wailing, might have been able to hear, from the back of their muddled minds, the talking drums at their funerals back home in their various villages, sounding:

Toppled Cornerstones, We Sympathize With You!

In the end, millions of the African population ended up as chattel slaves in the North Atlantic regions. However, after this "commodity" trading had been used to lay concrete foundations for the Industrial Revolution in Europe and the Americas, actions to stop chattel slave trading were taken in

1807 by the British, and in 1819 by North America. The Danish-Norwegian Kingdom passed a law to cease the trading a few years before Britain passed its law.

This was after nearly four centuries of European trading, involving popes, pastors, empires, kingdoms, Christian organizations, distinguished statesmen and women, medical doctors, and individual Christians - either directly, or through investment in chattel slave trading companies and their activities. Although slaves were released from their official status at the end of this trading, many of these freed slaves were bound up in their unfortunate status for a long time after the trade was officially abolished.

Even after these official abolitions, chattel slave trading continued unofficially until late in the 19th Century. Various historians have estimated how many Africans were captured in this deadly trade. Some historians have estimated that 90 million African slaves died on journeys to the various castles and forts, in the dungeons, or during shipment, and that about 45 million slaves reached the Americas. Some historians have calculated that, all in all, this amounted to 30% of Africa's population. Out of these numbers, it has been calculated that 12% were older children, 56% were men and 32% were women. Therefore, the ratio was two males to one female shipped, as some of the older children were girls.

There are only scanty historical accounts about female chattel slaves or those left behind. On the other hand, some historians argue that, since women are generally not as physically strong as men, most of the 90 million slaves who died in transit might have been women, girls and young children. Different historians give different calculations. Many travelers and historians did not take any interest in women's affairs, and therefore did not write much about women.

Further information about how women were treated in the over-crowded cabins during the voyage to the New World -

how they were raped constantly; how the sick, the difficult ones and the dead were thrown to the sharks; how these slaves were mercilessly beaten; and their inhuman existence in the Americas and in the Caribbean - all this information is beyond the scope of this book.(49) (50)

The following chapter offers a short summary of how this tragic chattel slave trade, conducted in West Africa by Christian Europe, affected the heritage of the women left behind on the Guinea Coast, especially the Akan tribe's women.

Picture 5: Slaves Being Disciplined On Their Way

Picture 6: Worthless Toddlers And Babies Being Thrown To Hyenas To Eat

Picture 7: Chattel Slaves Being Rowed To The European Slave Traders Ships

Picture 8: European Slaves Buyer Choosing His "Commodities"

Picture 9: An European Chattel Slave Trader Bidding For "Commodities"

CHAPTER 9

THE AKAN WOMEN LEFT BEHIND

There is a tragic question here: what happened to the other Akan women, the other toppled cornerstones left behind on the Guinea Coast after some of them were shipped away?

I am concentrating mainly on Akan women in this chapter, because the Akan were among the few West African ethnic groups who again resisted the patriarchal descent system brought to the Guinea Coast by European Christians. These were the same people who colonized and Christianized the Guinea Coast tribes after their chattel slave trading activities were over. The Akan had earlier fled the influence of Islam, including the patriarchal descent system introduced into the Western Sudan, where the Akan had previously lived in the Ghana Empire.

As already mentioned elsewhere in this work, the Akan clan groups held fast to their matriarchal descent family system, in which women were the cornerstones or foundation stones of their clans and maintained complementary relationships with their men. The Akan inherited their social status from their mothers. Therefore, women and men had great respect for each other, although ultimately this tradition was weakened by chattel slave trading, colonialism and the Christian religion. Another reason for focusing on Akan women is that some Akan groups sent armies which included women supporters to the Guinea Coast, to raid the castles and forts built along the coast by Christian chattel slave traders. Finally, I have chosen the Asante women from the Akan group, because the Asante had to fight the British colonialists, whose armies invaded the Asante and other Akan regions north of the coast to colonize and Christianize them, and some Asante queens and women were involved in these invasions.

There is not much in European written historical sources about Akan women's traditional status on the Guinea Coast during and immediately after the chattel slave trading period, apart from some scanty information about a few queen mothers. This is because, in the various cultures of the male Christian European chattel slave dealers, the European travelers along the Guinea Coast, and the historians who wrote initial histories of the African chattel slave trade, women did not have the same social status and attention as men. Therefore, some scholars argue that West African women's affairs were completely ignored on purpose, as such information would have embarrassed the Western civilized Christians back home, or undermined their religious principles. Therefore, the works of those early European writers were limited by their religious bias, as well as their cultural and gender bias.

However, most of the limited information in European sources about chattel slave trading, colonization and Christianization is cast positively as "West Africa's golden age".(51) In the same way, there is only limited written information about the origins of the Akan of present-day Ghana. After migrating to the ancient Gana (Ghana) Empire, where they lived between 300 CE and 1200 CE, they migrated again southwards towards the shores of the Guinea Coast. An elaborate and honest written history by the Europeans about this period of history, during which West African women were very powerful, would be interesting but sadly does not exist. However, a powerful ancient oral history tradition survives to this day.

While a few modern historians do not agree that the ancient Ghana Empire is connected to the modern Republic of Ghana in this way, some other modern historians do agree. They argue that the scholars from ancient West African kingdoms and empires wrote their own history when they moved from the Nile Valley to North and Western Sudan, and that these materials were deliberately destroyed by the Muslim Arab traders of salt, gold and slaves, who then introduced their religion in those regions from around 850 CE.

The newly-arrived Arab foreigners included geographers and historians, such as Ibn Munabbah, Ibn Khaldum, Abul Fida and Abd al-Rahman, who started to write the history of West Africa as they observed it from their own cultural perspectives. Therefore, some modern scholars argue that any concrete written proof of this connection between the migrants to ancient West Africa and the Nile Valley regions may have been deliberately destroyed. However, there is still a little written evidence from a few Arab and native writers, as well as from old oral history. Some artifacts and rock paintings also confirm this connection. There is only scanty written information about the position held by ancient West African women before the invasion of all the foreigners who came to those regions of Africa.

But regarding women's affairs in general, to this day, women are side-lined in many ways, not only in West Africa but throughout the world. Western women, have been fighting for more than a century now, and yet have still not reached full equality with their men. Besides their queens, only a small percentage of high positions in society - for example, in politics, commerce and industries and academic professions - are held by women.

Therefore, due to Western European ancient traditions and their Christian belief system, as well as their political activities, the Christian chattel slave traders, missionaries and colonial masters unfortunately did not take proper interest in women's affairs on the Guinea Cost when they arrived. The result is that, as already mentioned, there is only scanty original historical information about women's affairs on the Guinea Coast during the nearly 400 year period that Europeans were present on the Guinea Coast as masters.

A few of the women that these foreign historians wrote about, much later on, were great warrior queens of the Asante Kingdom: Yaa Asantewaa the Edwesohemaa, Ama Seewaa, and Kokofuhemaa Ataa Birago. These Queens together with their Kings sent Asante battalions to go and fight the British Colonial army invaders in the 19th Century, but this is more or less recent history.[52]

Eventually, the circumstances of those Akan women who were left behind after the slave trade were not better than those of the chattel slave women on their way to the new world. The women who were left behind suffered irreparable psychological, economic and cultural damages, as they were affected by the fact that most of them lost their husbands, brothers and sisters, children, mothers, and so on. These women left behind therefore had to take certain decisions that would normally be made together with the closely-knitted family or clan. Also, they had to do very hard and dangerous physical work, causing much damage to themselves, from the onset of that unusual type of slave trading throughout the introduction of colonization and Christianization.

Most of the men left behind were older men or disabled men. Consequently, the few able young men left behind and the elderly men had to marry many women in order to stabilize the population. As has already been mentioned elsewhere in this book, before the arrival of the Almoravid "jihads" between the 9th and 11th Centuries in West Africa, polygamy was practiced only by kings and a few people of high class for specific purposes; for example, to make tribal alliances to prevent wars. There is various evidence showing that polygamy was rare in ancient West Africa. For example, the couple - that is, a husband and wife in a monogamous relationship, as opposed to polygamous relationships - was positively reflected in the artwork of commoners before the 11th Century CE.

Even though polygamy was practiced by kings, chiefs and people of high class in their societies for specific purposes, it was not acceptable to the commoners. Evidence of hatred of polygamous relationships amongst ancient West African societies can be found in ancient pictorial and sculptural representations. Another interesting evidence of this however, is the linguistic evidence from many of the West African languages indicating the general disapproval of polygamy in their societies. For example:

> "Among the Igbo of Nnobi, for example, the suffix denoting the relationship one has with one's father - group's relatives, and siblings in a polygamous household is -nna ("father"), the same suffix is attached to words meaning "distrust," "suspicion," "greed," "jealousy," and "envy". In contrast, words dealing with trust, respect and love carry suffixes with the word for mother, nne."(53)

On the other hand, polygamous practices have been a widespread acceptable phenomenon in many West African countries since the breakup of the Ancient Western Sudan, including the Ancient Ghana Empire.(54)

This polygamous relationships practiced by those left behind on the Guinea Coast after the chattel slave trading did not seem to have helped much. The population kept on decreasing, despite the increase in polygamous practices to enable the single young women left behind to have many children and enrich their clans' populations. Furthermore, polygamy brought special problems for both men and women in their societies. Many of the women and men had no choice but to marry people from other tribes and cultures; in the old days, such marriages were pure gambling because of cultural differences, and therefore most of them did not last.

Other problem faced by these left-behind women affected them psychologically, economically, and culturally. First, farming activities decreased, affecting the economic situation of their societies. For example, the clearing and burning of the forest with large trees, and other heavy work that the men used to do to make the fields ready for cultivation, decreased. Next, the complicated large-scale group fishing "Kwagyan" (in one of the Akan dialects) activities that used to provide enough fish for local consumption, as well as for sale, also decreased, as did hunting activities to provide meat for their families and for sale. There was also a fall in men's special woodcarving and metalwork, and the production of beautiful metal artifacts sold to the Berbers and the Arab traders coming from the Sahara Desert area. The weaving activities of the spectacular and colorful "Kente" cloth - the patterns and the colors of which symbolically represented the various clans in this Akan group - also almost came to a standstill. Special deep-pit gold mining and gold washing activities, which used to produce gold for the trading with the Phoenicians and the Carthaginians that started long before the chattel slave traders arrived, also almost came to a standstill, as most of the strong men had been sold off, or these traders eventually preferred buying human beings to gold.

The result of this preference was that more captured slaves, including strong young men and women, were needed for sale in order that those men left behind could get their alcoholic drinks, which they became addicted to, and also their weapons to fight in order to capture more slaves. In the end, this type of slave trading activities, in that part of the Guinea Coast which became The Gold Coast and is now Ghana, became a vicious circle until the slave trading "officially" was abolished, for example, by the Danish-Norwegian Kingdom a few years before the British abolished theirs in 1807, followed by America and other European countries, like France, in 1817. However, as mentioned above, this trade continued unofficially for a long time in the 19th Century.

Finally, this trading of chattel slaves as commodities on the Guinea Coast affected these Guinea Coast women so badly that family systems broke down. Women had to do the hard physical work that men used to do in order to exist. The upbringing of children was now left mostly to women alone. Women and children lost their fathers, sisters, brothers, husbands, sons, daughters and other family members. All the people left behind in towns and in villages, especially the women, young people and children, were therefore affected psychologically, physically, mentally and economically. Customs and traditions also broke down. These activities, over a period of almost 400 years, left a deep scar on West African women's souls that can never be wiped off, as these women and their men left behind entered a new era in their existence: colonization of the Gold Coast.

Picture 10: Ancient West African Villagers Dancing To Mourn The Shipped Relatives

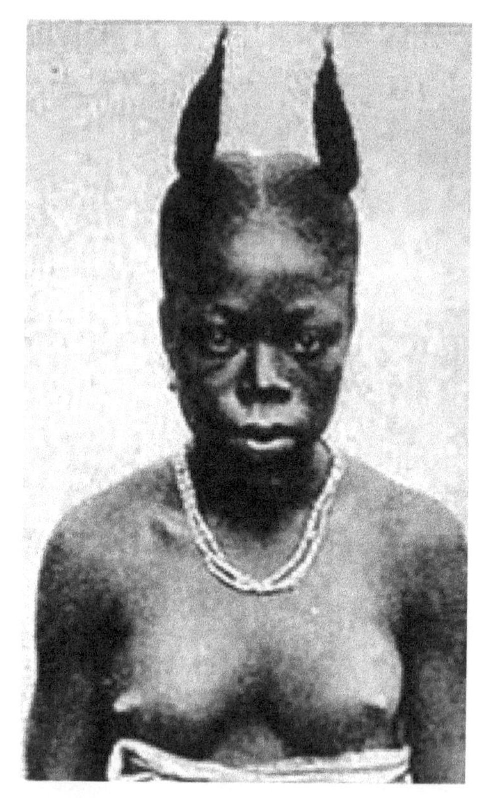

Picture 11: A Young Ancient West African Woman

Picture 12: Akan Young Women, Early 20th Century

Picture 13a: Akan Females At A Ceremony

Picture 13b: Modern Ghanaian Women In Ancient Kente Clothing

PART 3

CHAPTER 10

THE GOLD COAST

a. Colonization in General on the Guinea Coast

b. The Colonization of West Africa's Gold Coast

a. Colonization in General on the Guinea Coast

As already mentioned, Christian Europe's first contact with West Africa was in the 15th Century CE, whereas Arab Muslims arrived in North Africa between the 9th and 11th Centuries CE, bringing Islam together with their merchandise and their engagement in slave trading. However, in this study, as already mentioned, I will not deal with the Muslim Arab traders who were the first to come from the Middle East to the northern part of West Africa; neither will I go into details of the Christian European colonization and Christianization activities on the Guinea Coast. A full history of these activities is beyond the scope of this book.

During this time that these Christian Europeans were active in the area, from the middle of the 15th Century through to the 19th Century, their activities were confined to the coastal regions. At first they bought gold and spices on a small scale, but then later on their activities were concentrated mainly on buying slaves, the "human commodity" or "Black Gold", and selling their alcoholic drinks, guns and ammunition to the natives. One of the most important reasons that they remained near the coast was the political situation caused by the spread of Islam in the north, and the nature of Western Christianity.

In those days, Islam's power spread across the eastern and southern shores of the Mediterranean Sea and the Iberian Peninsula, creating a strong barrier between Europe and Africa and other parts of the world. But the problem was not just the influence of Islam in that area, but the fact that the Muslims actually ruled the Iberian Peninsula: both the Christian Europeans and the old Jewish Migrants who lived there were their subjects and had strict restrictions imposed on them, from the year 711 CE. However, by the year 1130 their rule started to decline and so they turned to the northwestern regions of Africa for their next occupation. Thus, Muslim occupation and rule of the Iberian Peninsula officially ended in 1492.

For this reason, now Christian Portugal and Spain were strong enough to develop their countries' economies independently. So Portugal started to recruit workers from Europe, as well as sailing southwards to explore the possibilities of slave labor from Africa. First, these ships explored to the islands along the coast of West Africa, captured Africans as slaves and brought them back to Portugal. Eventually, Christopher Columbus - a young laborer from Genoa, Italy, who had come to Portugal to look for work - was employed as a sailor and, with his Portuguese ship-mates, sailed south towards the West African coast. Eventually, they reached the Guinea Coast to start chattel slave trading, that is, the buying of humans as "commodities". Later, other Christian European chattel slave traders joined in this lucrative commercial activity.

As the result, when these natives of the Guinea Coast became confused and demoralized, some Christian European traders imposed colonial rule and their Christian

Religion in some parts of the Guinea Coast. This covered a region which was occupied by many tribes with various languages and dialects, different cultures and religions, and varied ways of dressing. That part of the Guinea Coast that was occupied by the British was eventually christened the "Gold Coast", because of the abundance of gold in the geological content of the region.

The British Empire officially abolished its chattel slave trading in 1807, a few years after the Danish-Norwegian Kingdom had officially abolished its trade. As a result, some freed slaves settled in the other newly-created British colonies of Sierra Leone and Liberia, to the west of the Gold Coast. A few years later, other Europeans followed suit, such as France in 1817, which also occupied some parts of West Africa and ruled the natives.[55] Overall, therefore, paradoxically, the abolition of this type of slavery did not set these African natives free. Instead, it led to the scramble for territories in West Africa because of the area's natural wealth. Besides gold, there were other precious metals, as well as products from its tropical forest and its animals. In the end, these resources led to the creation of many Christian European colonies in the southern area of West Africa.

Finally, now, the Europeans felt that the time was right for colonizing and Christianizing the West Africans on the Guinea Coast, who were completely confused and demoralized. Women, the cornerstones of their societies, became helpless: the old cultural order changed, as women were forced by their male Christian European masters to obey men in general, and also not to expect complementary existence with their own men anymore. Now these confused women, whether converted Christians or not, had to obey their men, as well as beg for help from men in everything.

So what happened to the relationship between mothers and their male children in the early days of colonial rule after the chattel slave trading? Once grown up, did men continue to have respect for their old mothers? This question reminds me of two interesting incidents I heard when I was conducting anthropological field work in Ghana about twenty-five years ago, regarding the great respect that mothers receive from their grown-up sons.

In the first incident, a man was walking past a kindergarten and saw many little children playing. The children asked him, "Where are you going?"

The man answered them, "I am going to see my sick mother."

The children started to laugh aloud and then replied, "But you are too big to have a mother. Mothers have only children."

The man responded, "Yes, I know, but I am her child; I will always be her child, it does not matter how big I have become. As a grown-up man, I love and respect my mother still."

A bell then rang instantly, and the confused little children ran back to their classroom, laughing at the big man who says he is a child of his mother.

In a another incident, I was told, a man was walking on a street somewhere, very depressed and looking like a vagabond. An old school friend he had not seen for many years suddenly met him and exclaimed, "My Goodness! Is that you, Frank? I have not seen you for a long time. What has happened to you?"

"Yes, James, it's me. Everything has fallen apart in my life," Frank answered him.

Looking a bit disturbed, James asked, "You know something Frank? Do you have a mother?"

"Yes, I have," answered Frank.

Then James said to him: "Go back home to your mother and blame her, say that it's all her fault that your life has collapsed. She will feel very sorry for you, comfort you and give you moral support, no matter what you say to her, as a mother always loves her children. It does not matter how big or how old they are, or how much these children blame them, as mothers always remember also their grown-up children as helpless babies. Go and do that, blame her! Then you will feel much better and have the courage to start life all over again, as you now have somebody to blame for your unfortunate life's condition that you have caused yourself. That's what mothers are for - kind, patient, sympathetic, no matter how old you are or how badly you treat them. They care! That's why we have to respect our mothers."

Frank answered, "What about a father?"

"You will be lucky, very lucky indeed, if you know hundred percent who your father is! Only mothers know!"

I will now return to the negative influence of colonialism on West African cultures and their tradition of complementarity between men and women, considering especially whether mothers do have problems of disrespect with their grown-up sons. I was once told by a group of women I met in inland Ghana during a local celebration that it is well known that sons from all walks of life always show great respect and love for their own mothers, the wombs from which they emerged. Paradoxically, however, when men act together collectively dealing with women, they always consider themselves superior to women, in accordance with the colonial mentality, as well as with Christian and Muslim religious cultures. I asked them whether they were sure of what they were saying. They laughed and said, "As women, we know men better than they know themselves. They came from our wombs!"

Well, I made no comment, so as not to upset these women from all walks of life, who were of different age groups, and had fathers, husbands, brothers and children themselves. They must have known what they were talking about.

Now, I come back to the introduction of Christian European colonialism after the chattel slave trade, after which a great revolution started on the Guinea Coast. The great order, in which males respected women, was disrupted. Islam's influence started to move southwards towards the Guinea Coast in the 1770s. Meanwhile, the British, Dutch, French, Prussians and Swedes, the Danish-Norwegian Kingdom, and the other Christian European chattel slave traders "officially" stopped their trading in humans and concentrated on their scramble to colonize and Christianize the various kingdoms and empires along the Guinea Coast in the 19th Century. All these changes finally and permanently eradicated West African women's position as cornerstones in their societies, as well as their complementary existence with their men.[56]

b. The Colonization of West Africa's Gold Coast

On 6 March 1957, the Gold Coast became the first black African colony of the British Empire to be granted independence. Long before 1901, the British gave the name "Gold Coast" to an area just along the Guinea Coast, but this area was not occupied by just one ethnic group of people. The Christian British occupied this whole area, which had many different ethnic groups of people, with many different cultures, languages and dialects, styles of dress, food, and ways of contacting the Creator God. The colonialists formed one country, and named it the "Gold Coast" because of the abundance of gold deposits in the region's geology underground, as mentioned above.

As time passed, this British colony of the Gold Coast was forcefully expanded; eventually, many other kingdoms and states, large and small, stretching along the Coast and northwards towards the savannah, were also included in the Gold Coast colony. These included the Asante Kingdom and various ethnic states and kingdoms in the northern part of the Guinea Coast, which also consisted of several ethnic and linguistic groups; all were forced to be part of the British Empire's Gold Coast colony. Part of Togoland, which was initially colonized by the Germans, was also drawn into the Gold Coast colony.

But the British government did not find it easy to colonize the area. Many of these tribes resisted colonization. For example, while trying to bring the Asante Kingdom under the rule of the Gold Coast colony rule, the British fought two wars in the Asante region around Kumasi, their capital town: the Sagrenti war in 1874, and the Yaa Asantewaa war in 1900. Unfortunately, the Asante lost. In the end, the Christian British Empire Colonialists managed to combine the various states and kingdoms within their Gold Coast colony, which was ruled from thousands of miles away, by their Parliament in London.

Therefore, when the Gold Coast was granted independence, it was necessary to form a new nation, with over forty languages, innumerable dialects (some of which no longer exist) a new name to satisfy each of the numerous ethnic groups and cultures. Eventually, the name Ghana was chosen, the name of the legendary, powerful empire in the ancient Western Sudan on the Savanna, from where most of these ethnic groups had migrated southwards because of the pressure from the Muslims to the north. After independence, Dr. Kwame Nkrumah became the first elected Prime Minister, on 6 March 1957. In 1960, the country became a Republic, but remained a member of the British Commonwealth of Nations.

After chattel slave trading, colonialism brought even more confusion to the demoralized Guinea Coast women, as this new order brought more strange culture to them. They now had to respect their men and obey them. Those few females who had the opportunity to go to school had to behave and dress like women back home in Europe. European "ladies'" dresses were to be worn, with high-heeled shoes, stockings, gloves and hats for church, parties and special occasions, even though the heat sometimes reached over 40 degrees centigrade in some parts of the country. West African women also had to learn to cook and eat European dishes with their families, to be eaten with knives, forks and spoons. These dishes included the British breakfast dish of bacon and eggs, made with bacon and the fresh eggs imported from Britain. When West African women followed these strange traditions, then they qualified as "ladies", compared to those women who did not go to school and were therefore viewed as backward and primitive illiterates.

But the confusion did not end with the Colonialism. There was a new order that came hand in hand with the colonialism to bring more confusion for the women. That was the introduction of Christian culture and its patriarchal descent system.

Picture 14: The Akan " Asesedwa" And The Famous Akan " Kente" Cloth

CHAPTER 11

THE CHRISTIANIZATION OF WEST AFRICA'S GOLD COAST

"The Berlin Conference of 1884 to 1885 accelerated the scramble for Africa, so that the 1904 inter-mission conference set in motion the scramble for spheres of influence among the missions."(57)

"In December 1828 the first Basel missionaries arrived at Christiansborg Castle, the Danish headquarters on the Gold Coast. Six years later the first Wesleyan missionaries reached Cape Coast. Though they attracted little attention at the time, these two events turned out to be as important as some of the more stirring events of European contact with the country."(58)

"Even though the English, Danish and Dutch establishments on the Coast usually had a Chaplain among their trading officers, their work was limited to their own Europeans, their mulatto wives and their children."(59)

Portuguese Christian missions first brought Christianity to West Africa. However, this mission work was only for their own chattel slaves and gold traders at their trading posts in some parts of the West African coast. These limited missionary activities for their own traders and their mulatto children continued, on and off, from 1482 to 1576. However, in 1576, all the Catholic Missionaries who arrived on the

Coast and started to work in the Komenda area, on the Guinea Coast, were massacred by the natives.(60)

Once, when I was doing my anthropological field work in that region, I had an informal conversation with some of the natives about this massacre. They told me that they had heard from their own oral history (called "mpanyinsem" in one of the Akan dialects) that those people who performed the massacre were unconsciously retaliating to what was happening to them. These village people argued that the misuse of West African female chattel slaves in the dungeons of the Christian European castles and forts, the export of women by white Christian traders, and the sacrifices made by those disillusioned West African women left behind, had laid the foundations for Western Christian civilization and its excessive material wealth. These villagers argued that the worst possible insult and blow to West Africa was the introduction of Western materialist values, at the same time that the trade of chattel slaves or "Black Gold" was coming to an end, and West Africa was being colonized and Christianized by these same former chattel slave traders.

Therefore, these villagers continued that, the introduction of Christianity on the Gold Coast by the Christian Colonialists was not at all easy, hence the massacre. They continued to argue that, their women were downgraded by these European Christian Missionaries, and therefore, did not care much about their welfare. For example, the West African women who had the great luck to have a little Western type of education as stated above had to follow European women's way of life and ignore their cultural heritage.(61)

While listening to these unusual arguments of these villagers, I was also told that, in the past, females in the Gold Coast were not encouraged to have higher education like the males because the European Christian missionaries reasoned that, whatever a woman's education, she would always end up in the kitchen, just like their own women back home in Europe. Therefore, in those days, the few West African women who were able to have a little formal higher education faced a great risk of never finding husbands. These same missionaries educated their countrymen back home, and discouraged them from having highly-educated wives. Otherwise, if educated African husbands had wives with good education like themselves, how could they control their wives as was done in the Christian Europe in those days? However, these villagers continued to argue that, nowadays in modern Ghana, men are very proud of their well-educated mothers, wives, sisters, daughters and other female relatives.

Other observers of cultural developments in West Africa argue that Western-style formal education in West Africa made a great contribution and helped the entire old order to change. Even though, the old matriarchal descent system somehow existed on the surface among some tribes, the complementary existence between females and males disappeared forever. In the end, the patriarchal descent system brought by these Missionaries ruled, even when the matriarchal descent system of inheritance existed just on the surface.

But the confusion of the Gold Coast's women under the rule of Western European Christian culture did not end there. Further confusion was caused by their chance for a little formal, western-style education. Most of the West African women who went to school got confused in many ways. For example, some of the educated women wanted to look like white European women, by lightening their black skin and straightening their beautiful black curly hair, so that they would be attractive to their equally confused Black educated men. For this reason, lots of chemicals imported from the "civilized" Christian Western world were used on the skin of educated West African women, in some cases causing skin cancers and other serious skin diseases. In addition, as well as using chemicals to straighten their hair, black West African women sometimes used glowing hot iron combs and other heated devices to straighten their beautiful black curly hair, to look like white Christian European women.

When I discussed this phenomenon with women during my research travels in West Africa, many of them argued that, even up to this 21st Century, the show goes on! The confusion goes on! Many black women in Africa, as well as some black women living in the Western world, continue to use deadly chemicals to whiten their skin, in order to look like European women. Many chemicals are also used on their hair to make it long and straight like white women's. On the other hand, nowadays, some of the long hairs are wigs, or European or Asian hair woven into these black women's natural curly hair.

Once, during one of my anthropological fieldwork this time in the UK, I went to a black women's hairdressing salon. I asked one of the African hairdressers there where all those long European-style wigs in their salon came from - whether they were artificial, or whether they were genuine hair from living or dead people. She answered that she did not know, and that all that she knew was that they were genuine human hair; she said they were probably not from dead people, but she was not sure.

However, it was at this moment in this same hairdresser's salon that a rather serious argument developed concerning how Western Christian missionaries in West Africa looked down on the women there, concerning their way of dressing and so forth. Eventually the argument changed course and touched on other subjects. For example, one of the discussion topics was how the missionaries blamed the "heathens" for performing human sacrifices. I noticed that one young woman, one of two African university students who had come to the salon to have their modern European hairstyles re-done, was wearing black dress. I became curious about her black clothes, even though I did not know her nationality. In the culture of the Akan of West Africa, wearing black clothes is a sign of mourning a dead person. Therefore, I asked her, sympathetically, where she came from and who had died in her family. Incidentally, she happened to be from one of the eight Akan ethnic groups of Ghana, and had come to Britain to study. She told me that it was her grandfather, "my mother's father, who was a Divisional Chief back home". I asked her how her grandmother, one of the Divisional Chief's wives, was coping with this loss, and she answered that she was coping quite well.

Then I told them some oral history regarding some ancient West African cultures. For example, in those days, polygamy was not a common practice; however, if a paramount chief or an important chief with more than one wife died, his beloved first wife would usually volunteer to accompany her husband back to the ancestors in the Spirit World. Then, this wife would die mysteriously, and would be buried side by side with her dear husband. Also, many material things such as gold nuggets, clothes, cooking utensils, water jugs, or serving earthenware bowls would also be placed in the private graveyard of this important person. Such a way of life, I continued, amounted to human sacrifice; even though the practice was voluntary, the missionaries opposed it and some people admired them for this.

At this point, the whole salon became a debate parlor. One of the students started to lecture us, saying:

> "Human sacrifice, or the killing of human beings in different ways for different reasons, has been taking place all over the world since human beings started to settle down properly 10,000 years ago, and has been continuing

even after the introduction of religions such as Christianity - a fact that many historians will not dispute. To this day, human beings are being killed in wars, or as murderers in prisons, in this civilized world. The worse part of this human weakness is "infanticide", that is, getting rid of unwanted children in various ways. This practice took place, for example, in ancient Rome, Greece, Mesopotamia, and many other places in Europe. Unfortunately, this practice is still taking place in this, our modern world, in many different ways. The worst type of infanticide in today's Christian, civilized, modern Western world is "abortion". In most of Western countries today, a pregnant woman can go to her doctor and say, I am pregnant, but I do not want a child now. Then the living and breathing fetus will be removed a live and thrown away. However, I have heard that some highly developed people, who are religious but not Christians, argue that, the very moment a male sperm comes into contact with the female egg, there is a soul or a being involved. Therefore, to these people, such an abortion is murder, just like the infanticide of ancient times. These people argue that modern humans, including Christians and other religious people, try to solve the symptom, that is, abortion, without tackling the true problem: how to have a purposeful sex at the right time and for a specific purpose. This is because, in so far as human species have to continue to exist in this dimension, children have to be born from sexuality. These people also argue that, from ancient times to this day, many babies and children continue to be abandoned or killed in Christian Europe, which amounts to infanticide."

This student at last paused for a few seconds, and before her listeners could put questions to her, she continued her strange argument. She said that, in this civilized, modern, Christian Western world, fetuses are also sorted. Some of us listening to her lecture asked her how. She explained again that nowadays, when a woman becomes pregnant, she can go to a doctor to check whether she will be having a girl or a boy. If the result shows a boy and she does not want a boy, then she will simply go and have an abortion to get rid of the developing human baby. In the same way, if the test shows a girl and she does not want a girl, she goes in for an abortion. This student ended her talk by saying that she was a Christian herself, but sometimes she wondered what would have been our Great Prophet Jesus Christ's advice or recommendation about this modern type of infanticide, including abortion. However, as He did not write the Bible Himself we cannot get clear guidance. In the end, women are the culprits, not the medical doctors doing their jobs.

At this time, all of us who were listening to this student became very surprised; whether we agreed with what she was saying or not, we had serious food for thought. Even those customers who came in to buy cosmetics stopped and listened. Some thought that the student was making it up, but those customers who knew Christian Western countries well agreed with what this student of Church History was telling us. I was speechless.

The second student, who was studying Medicine, also talked about how her chosen profession is becoming more and more advanced and exciting in this civilized Christian Western world. In connection with her claim, she told us more frightening stories about medical advancement in our modern times. She was also thinking about the civilized Western Christian world, where "spare parts" of humans who are still breathing but declared "brain dead" are removed from their bodies, just before they stop breathing to die, and are used as transplants for other people. She also talked about how the removed human fetuses are being used in many ways. She told us how in some cases, while surgeons are preparing to take the human parts they need from unconscious patients, then suddenly, some of these patients in coma, who are declared "brain dead", would start to move their eyes, which is a sign of waking up. At this point this student told us a strange but serious joke, offering food for thought, which she had heard about human spare parts transplants. This is her story.

> Once, there were four people sitting closely together on a train from London to Edinburgh in the UK. They did not know each other, but somehow they became engaged in a lively conversation about the amazing advancement of modern medical transplantation technology in the Christian Western world. One of these men told the others a story of how a man, through a very serious accident, lost many parts of his body, but did not die. In the end the doctors decided to do their best for him. So first he was given a new leg and a new arm, to replace his amputated leg and arm. He was then given a new brain from a dying young woman, a new heart from a dying young girl, and a new kidney from a young boy who had just had a bicycle accident and was in coma. Then he also received a new liver from another young woman dying from some strange inherited disease. Finally, he was given a facial transplant from a donation from the family of a dying man, who had fallen off his roof-top and had been in coma for a long time.
>
> The listeners were very amazed and some were frightened. But then one of the passengers sitting behind this group, who had also been listening to this unusually strange story, asked the storyteller, "You know something, I should like to know something. Are you all Christians?"

"Yes, we are," all of them answered. The man continued, "I should like to know: what will happen to this man, who received so many spare parts from so many people, when he dies? In accordance with the Christian Holy Bible, when we all die we go and rest somewhere, and at the "Resurrection on the Judgement Day", all of us have to wake up from our resting places for our souls to face our Creator God, concerning how we have lived our lives in this dimension, that is, on Mother Earth. Which soul of these donators is this man going to represent?"

"In my opinion," he continued without waiting for an answer to his question, "First, there must be a limit to what should be transplanted. Second, in my opinion, only "living" family members or friends should be allowed to donate, because for a sick person to "wish" that somebody would die in order for him or her to live, is wrong. Third, a person could be in coma for some time, but then would suddenly wake up again. Therefore, to remove such a patient's organs is murder. In my opinion, people should be taught to be brave and accept their destiny, no matter whether a person came to this dimension for just, one day, 10 years, 50 years or 100 years, depending on your mission in this dimension. I strongly believe that life continues in other dimensions after physical death. Nowadays, we hear a lot about the serious corruption going on in the lucrative business of the sale of human spare parts. Some poor people in some countries get tricked to sell their spare parts for money. Some children round the world get kidnapped or are sold by criminals for their spare parts to be removed. Many prisoners in some countries are forced to donate their organs, and so on. Then, the big question is, who are these medical doctors who collaborate with these criminals? Therefore, in my opinion, much precaution has to be taken about human spare parts transplantation while Scientists are working hard to grow these "human spare parts" from scratch."

At last, this medical student finished her much more serious story regarding the conversation of those passengers traveling from London to Edinburgh. According to this student storyteller, when this man on the train had finished his argument about human transplant, he did not get an answer to his question concerning who would be represented on Judgement Day by the soul of the man who had received multiple human organ transplants.

Again, according to this Student, some other people listening just laughed, and others made no comment; but that one woman, sitting somewhere behind these people on the train, thought the man's question about Judgement Day was good question. So this woman asked the man whether he was a pastor or belonged to some sort of religious group. On the other hand, one man on the train praised modern medical technology, saying that, in his opinion, if a healthy person wants to donate his or her entire body to a sick person, such a donation should be accepted. But others argued that, such a donation would amount to murder or suicide.

At last, this medical student finished her serious "joke story" about the advancement of modern medical technology, which was being discussed on a fast train in the UK. However, some of the customers in the salon who had been listening to her did not think that her story was a joke to be laughed at.

Eventually, the discussions of this strange gathering, at this strange place in a hairdresser's salon, became more serious and frightening. As one of the women having her hair done, she also expressed her fear that, unlike the ancient West African women's complementary existence with their men,

Western men are jealous of women because of the simple fact that all men, noble or ordinary, came from a woman's womb, and therefore might welcome another strange medical technology. She continued to say that a day might come when babies might be hatched in incubators, as chickens were hatched from eggs some time ago in the 20th Century. That is, women's eggs and men's sperms, she argued, could be put into incubators to hatch babies. A person, man or woman, who would like to buy a baby would then fill in a form, specifying color of skin, eyes and hair, height and weight, blood type, and so on, each of which could be paid for. Then after some months, the babies would be "hatched" ready to be delivered to their "parents". All this would degrade women of their pride that every man came from a woman's womb, a fact that the missionaries of the Western Christianity ignored when they came to West Africa, leading to the degradation of the West African women's position in their societies.

The group of people in the salon who had been listening to this tale of "incubated babies" said that such a period in human history would be the end of our human species as we know it today. Some said that probably, our souls would then be taken over by "alien beings" in the incubators, and that such "beings" would behave differently, and then quickly get rid of us, the old strange decaying species.

What a day! I said to myself. What made me enter this salon today?

In short, up to the 20th Century, the effects of the North Atlantic chattel slave trade, Western colonization, and the Western Christian mission work based on patriarchal descent system destroyed West African women's complementary existence with their men, and also left other deep scars on West African women. One such scar is the copying of white European women's looks, as discussed above. Instead of West African women copying the white Western women's hairstyles to look like white women in black skin, black women could have developed their old traditional beautiful hairstyles: beautiful African woven or plaited styles to suit black skin. Or they could have developed the beautiful Akan queens and queen-mothers hairstyle, just cut short and beautiful. Similar development could have been applied to the beautiful West African women's traditional clothing.

However, according to traditional oral history, there were certain traditional practices in West Africa, involving both women and men, that the Western Christian missionaries could not do anything to change. One example is body decoration and tribal markings.

Some of the educated West African women copied the use of lipstick from the Western white women, but mouth decoration was not new in ancient West Africa. In some of the cultures in ancient West Africa, women decorated their bodies in various ways for particular situations: when there were special celebrations, or when an important person died, or when there was a catastrophe in their family or society. For example, women decorated their faces and bodies with special white or red clay on special ceremonial days, or after childbirth, or for special funerals. Also, tribal markings made with knives were very common, both as decorations and also for specific purposes. For example, some of the marks were for clan identification, for economic activities such as farming, fishing and craft work. Some offered protection from certain diseases, some were for secret spiritual clubs such as medicine women and men or witch doctors' clubs. Some of these marks were for identifying some royal family members, whereas others were just for decorating the body.

On the other hand, in some of the cultures, including some of the Akan tribes of West Africa, it was a serious taboo to use a knife on one's body, except in very special situations, such as for the prevention or cure of special diseases, or for some special Medicine Women or Men. Therefore, both female and male genital circumcision was, and is still, a great taboo in Akan culture. A circumcised person from a royal family could not become a chief, king or queen. However, even among those tribes where body scarification practices had been carried on as an important part of their culture, such practices are now slowly disappearing, which is a good thing as such practices had their own health problems.(62)

Generally speaking, the European Christian mission work in West Africa, could not influence these West African women's and men's traditional body decoration cultures much.

Now, the next stage - after the loss of West Africa women's ancient positive status in their societies through chattel slave trading, colonization and Christianization - is that West Africa is now being dragged into following the globalization of the Christian Western world's excessive materialism. It is therefore being graded according to this phenomenon. That is, Africa had been known as the dark, primitive, backward continent by the Christian Western World. Later on, Africa was promoted to the status of "Underdeveloped continent" and now, Africa is promoted again to the status of "developing Africa", with West African women still struggling at the bottom of their societies while they say goodbye to their lost status. This reminds me of a little funny story I heard when I was doing field work deep in the Savannah of West Africa, on the question of "underdevelopment". The following is the story.

> Once, three young village school girls, teenagers, were carrying earthenware pots on their heads in the bush just outside their hamlet, on their way to fetch water from a little stream. They were walking "topless", without blouses on, exposing their well-developed heavy breasts.

It was a normal practice for both men and women to go almost naked around in that region in those days, as the temperatures were sometimes between 40° and 45° Celsius all year round. However, if they had to go to school, hospital or church, or to any other official appointment, then they dressed fully.

On this occasion, while walking on the footpath just outside their hamlet, the girls met two newly-arrived male European Christian missionaries, coming from a neighboring village. These men became so confused at their encounter with the topless teenage girls that they kept on looking at their big, heavy and well-developed breasts. After these men had passed them, one of the girls asked her friends, "Why did they stare at us like that, I wonder?"

The second girl said, "They were looking not just at us, but at our breasts!"

Then the third girl said, "Yes, they call us Africans "under-developed" because we do not have thin breasts like their women. To them, anybody who does not have white skin like them, who does not eat the type of food they eat or wear the type of clothes they wear, and does not behave like them or have the same opinions as them, is "under-developed". It does not matter how well-developed a person's breasts are, how healthy a person's body is, or how high a person's education is."

Well, that was food for thought about "underdevelopment." Perhaps these newly-arrived European Christian missionaries later forced these villagers to wear proper clothes like Europeans, even in their homes, regardless of the temperatures.

Eventually, as Christianization in West Africa gathered momentum, so did the confusion in women's affairs.

CHAPTER 12

BOTH COLONIZATION AND CHRISTIANIZATION BROUGHT MORE CONFUSION FOR WEST AFRICAN WOMEN

To make matters worse for West African women, as already discussed, Christian European chattel slavery was followed immediately by colonialism and then by Christianization. Colonialism brought confusion amongst kingdoms and empires, languages and dialects; the introduction of Christianity, which came hand-in-hand with Colonialism, brought further confusion in West African cultures, this time amongst families and clans. Families, clans and ethnic social systems began to break up, as some family or clan members became Christians and others did not.

One simple example can be found in my mother's royal Akan Aduana clan, late in the 19th Century in the Gold Coast, when the spread of colonialism and Christianity in the Asante region led to wars between the Asante and the Christian Colonialists. According to this clan's old oral historians, the Aduana clan's family members were powerful traditional herbal medicine women and men, and some were spiritual healers and seers. Besides offering special help to people who consulted them in decision-making, these traditional medicine women and men could cure strokes, mental illnesses, snake bites, serious tropical boils, and bleeding or wounds caused by accidents. They were also able to solve most problems, of infertility, difficult childbirth, impotence, incontinence, and all types of fevers. They could also help the handful of people who complained that they felt sometimes dizzy and that, when they urinated, ants gathered to "drink" the urine. This disease could have been, in modern times, diabetes. Some of the fevers they were able to cure might have included the deadly malaria fever.

Now let us see how the introduction of Christianity in that part of the Guinea Coast of West Africa which became the Gold Coast seriously affected these medicine women and men.

To begin with, in those days, the sick villagers who had been converted to Christianity were strictly forbidden to go to these medicine women and men. The result was that, in those days, the sick villagers had to walk for many miles on foot, or be carried by family members, through deep forests, across large and deep rivers and over fallen trees, risking meeting lions or other wild and dangerous animals, to reach the nearest few little Christian European clinics. Sometimes, these sick villagers and their helpers had to go in very heavy tropical storms and lightning, which caused even the biggest trees to fall; or when temperatures were above 35° Celsius. And as some of the sick people were not strong enough to walk, or to be carried for such long distances, many died in their homes or on the way to these health posts.

The conditions described above show how these traditional herbalists and spiritual healers were of great help to their societies, especially during emergency situations such as poisonous snakebites, children's convulsion, sudden difficulties in childbirth, accidents, and so on. But, after colonization and Christianization, all this ancient health wisdom was forbidden for converted Christians, as traditional health workers were all branded "devils". The result was that many Christians, especially women and children, died in emergency cases, instead of getting help from their traditional health practitioners next-door. For this reason, many people now ask themselves: why did such useful Guinea Coast women bear the brunt of this strange mixture of chattel slave trading, colonization and the wrong way of introducing Christianity, resulting in the loss of ancient wisdom forever?

One day, during one of my field work travels in a remote Asante (Akan) village in Ghana, I interviewed a 95-year-old converted Christian woman, who was once a young priestess-healer and herbalist for one of the Akan ethnic group's lesser gods during the early 20th Century. I asked her how she and the other medicine women and men used to work before she became a Christian. This old woman was very physically strong and mentally alert for her age, so she was very keen to talk about how they used to work.

She told me that, before they started any treatment at all, a client would be told: "Se Onyankopon Pe a woho beye woden". In "Twi", one of the Akan ethnic group dialects, this means: "If it is the Will of the Almighty God, you will be cured." They would then pray to some ancestral spirits and lesser gods, asking them to take their requests to the Almighty God as intermediaries, to guide them to finding the right cure for the client. Also, they had special symbols at special places, like mountain sides, river banks, lake sides, special rocks, special trees, etc. There they would sacrifice hens, birds or animals to these lesser gods and ancestral spirits, asking for their help to mediate by contacting, on their behalf, The Creator God. In the same way, some Christians pray to God through Jesus Christ for help, asking some angels, or the Virgin Mary, mother of Jesus Christ, or some canonized outstanding figures from church history, to help them get their prayers through to God.

At this point, I asked her what happened to the dead hens and animals they sacrificed. She told me that they used to toast the meat on fire or cook it to eat in fellowship, so that everybody who attended such ceremonies took part in the feasting. It was at this moment that this 95-year-old woman posed two strange questions that frightened me. Her first question was as follows:

> "When we go to church and the pastor performs the Holy Communion ritual, that is, when he puts a piece of bread on our tongue to eat, he says that it is the flesh of Jesus Christ. When he gives us some wine to drink, he says it is the blood of Jesus Christ. Did the people there during the time of Jesus Christ eat human beings and drink human blood? The pastor never tells us the meaning of this symbolism. Maybe in those days, some of the cultures around that area where these white pastors came from might have had traditions in which human beings were sacrificed, and their flesh were eaten and their blood was drunk, as part of their worshipping traditions. What do you think is the meaning of this symbolism in Christianity?"

I was shocked, but then I said that even though I was a Christian, I did not know the meaning of this symbolism. Then her next question came.

> "About the Cross that we Christians wear, for example, if somebody kills your mother with an axe, do you have to wear an axe symbol all your life, which should have been a taboo in our culture? Can't you wear something else that your mother used to like, or some other positive symbol to remember her with, and also to give you encouragement in life?"

Again, I could not answer this question. She was a bit disappointed in my ignorance. However, both of us laughed and I said goodbye to her, and left very quickly to avoid more embarrassing religious questions.

On another occasion, in another town, a schoolteacher told me of an interesting experience he had just had. The story was as follows:

> Once a neighbor of his, a retired midwife, went to her farm just on the outskirts of their village. Unfortunately, she was bitten by a big poisonous snake; however, she managed to get to the roadside very quickly, and a kind man drove her to a hospital only a few miles away. She was at this point showing signs that her heart was stopping. She was treated without delay and sent home by the same car that took her there. Two hours later, her condition worsened. She started to show signs of her heart stopping again, and was slowly losing consciousness. Some neighbors who passed by decided to help her by contacting a local woman who was a traditional herbalist. This dying woman had no choice, as she was not conscious enough to say yes or no.
>
> Fortunately or unfortunately, this traditional herbalist had just delivered a baby only a few hours earlier, yet when she was contacted, she was able to get up to fetch some herbs, fresh from the bush just outside her house. She prepared them very quickly, and then gave this herbal medicine to her six-year-old daughter, with instructions regarding what to do and how to do it when she got to the dying woman. The little girl was accompanied by some grown-ups to the house of this dying retired midwife, and she performed the treatment exactly according to her mother's instructions. Within just ten minutes, this dying woman started to breathe deeply and then vomited, feeling very relieved. Also, due to another mixture that the little girl rubbed on the bitten leg, a sort of white powder-like stuff started to come out of the skin of the bitten leg. This retired midwife became conscious again and started to talk, asking what was

going on. She then thanked all the neighbors who had gathered there to help her, as well as the little six-year-old girl and the grown-ups who brought her there. This retired midwife was cured immediately.

However, later on, the neighbor who had helped this snake-bitten retired midwife said to me that he heard that this cured woman did not want to talk to people about the dangerous situation she had found herself in, and her miracle cure by the traditional herbal medicine woman. Otherwise, she would be banned from taking part in her church's Christian Holy Communion, for the simple reason that she got help from a herbal medicine woman who they called a "devil".

Unfortunately, all these ordinary traditional West African herbal medicine women and other spiritual medicine women were branded "witches" and "devils" by the European Christian missionaries. The result was that many people in need of help died, as many gifted traditional women healers abandoned their special gifts forever. Therefore, the confusion went on.

On another day, a very old man in a town I visited in that same area of my research work told me another interesting story, as an example of the wrong way that Christianity was introduced in their town early in the 20th Century. He told me his personal experience:

"When I was a child, our town was divided into two. One area, where the European Missionaries built their little church, became the area belonging to Jesus Christ's "good Christian people", and the other side of our town belonged to the heathens, that was, the "devil's evil people" who were not Christians. Therefore, those children living on the side of the converted Christians were told not to play with children on the heathens' side, although some of the people living in the "good Christian people's" area had close family members living on the "devil's" side. Also, even though some heathen parents in those days sent their children to the new Christian missionary school which had just been opened in our town, so that they would learn how to read and write, there were great difficulties. The few school children from the "devil's" side who had the opportunity to attend school, as well as those children who were not attending school also on the "devil's" side, could not play together with the schoolchildren from the side of "good Christian people". It was forbidden."

This old man continued his story:

"Eventually, the Christians were advised to always build their houses around their church's area. Furthermore, the Christians were barred from getting help from their local traditional herbalists, as well as from taking part in all the cultural and social festivities like drumming, singing, dancing and special social and cultural celebrations which were going on in our town, which had nothing to do with "heathen gods". Then, on top of all these prohibitions, the Christians had their own little cemetery, and the heathens also had theirs. However, the entrance of the non-Christians' cemetery had an inscription written by the European Christian missionaries, in "Twi", which read thus:

"Nea Onim Papa ye na wanye no, eye Bone ma no." That is, "He/She who knows what is Right and does not do it, is a Sinner." "

Looking back, this old man argued that it was wrong for those European Christian missionaries to judge people who were not converted Christians to be "devils". Therefore, they should not have written such a thing at the entrance of the non-Christian cemetery. Second, regarding traditional medicine, the missionaries could have asked those ordinary herbal medicine women and men who were not "spiritualists", and who wanted to join the Christian Church and at the same time help their people by continuing to practice their traditional healthcare practices with just herbs, to continue to work but only in the name of Jesus Christ. Then these herbalists could have asked for guidance from Jesus, the Virgin Mary or the angels, as the Christian clinics and hospitals were too far away from some of the little towns and villages for emergency cases. Unfortunately, instead, these traditional herbalists who were not spiritualists and who joined the Christian Church were branded "devils" and "witches". They therefore stopped their practices, and eventually knowledge of herbal medicine died out as it was not passed on to later generations. As most of those herbalists were women, in the end, women once again became the losers.

Eventually, the introduction of European Christianity brought chaos and more confusion amongst families, clans and societies. The converted Christians' ancestral heritage of great knowledge of healing herbal medicine, practiced by both the women and men, was abandoned as these gifted people, especially the converted women Christians, could not stand the great humiliation of being branded witches and devils.

Paradoxically, when I was later doing other anthropological field research in Ghana[63], many people told me about agents who today come from the Western World to West Africa, often under cover, to get information about West

African traditional herbal medicine on behalf of international medical companies.

As already mentioned, this book is not a detailed account of Christian missionary work in the Gold Coast immediately after the chattel slave trade and colonization. As I am mentioning only how the Western Christian religion backed this trading, I do not intend to describe in detail the work of the hundreds and hundreds of European Christian missionaries who flooded to the Gold Coast to work for the various European Christian churches, while some of their countries were planning how to get more and more benefits from their colonization of West Africa to enrich their countries.

During one of my research trips through the whole of Ghana, I talked to some local people at different places who had knowledge of the history of Christian European chattel slave trading on the Guinea Coast. It was strange that all of them, Christians and non-Christians alike, said they sometimes wonder whether the Christian Holy Bible that these white people's pastors brought and used to pray to God through Jesus Christ to bless their "human commodity" trading business was actually the same Holy Bible that is being used in this 21st Century by Christians all over the world.

Again, these people asked whether the Holy Bible of today is the same as the Holy Bible that those Christian European pastors used for praying to God through Jesus Christ, asking for the confused humans, the "human cargo'", in the dungeons of the slave ships', to arrive safely at the various markets in the Northern Hemisphere. In the end, these people asked me again and again whether the interpretation of the Christian Holy Bible has changed in these modern times.

Hence, the following are only a few comments of some historians of Christian mission work in the Gold Coast immediately after the chattel slave trading stopped, while colonization and Christianization were in progress.

Picture 15: The Asante King Being Followed By His Men To A Funeral In Kumase, The Capital Of The Asante Kingdom

CHAPTER 13

CHRISTIANIZATION'S CONFUSION CONTINUES

The following are just a few comments made by some historians of the church, concerning the introduction of Christianity to West Africa.

> "The main thrust of European Christian missionary activity was to "Christianize" Africa in the manner and fashion of the European appropriation of the Christian evangel; and much of the missionary endeavor was based on the presupposition that African ways were necessarily pagan and had to be done away with."(64)

> "There is a tendency by some historians to enter into West African Church history by focusing on activities in the mission fields to the utter neglect of the home base. Yet the stories of the various missions are so interwoven with the histories of the metropolitan countries from which they came that the pattern of missionary enterprise in the field can only be explained by reference to where from, how and why the missionaries came."(65)

> "It must be pointed out that upsurge of missionary activity in this period arose from many factors which are usually captioned with the slogan, "FOR GLORY, GOLD, AND GOD." The quest for political and military "glory" touched off the scramble for colonies and the need for stabilizing the presence of each

> Christian European power. The scramble was also for "Gold" and markets - a quest intensified by the industrial revolution and supported by the mixed mercantilist and free-trade theories. Philanthropic and evangelical groups sought to further God's divine economy. Thus, anti-slavers jostled with proponents of legitimate trade in advocating a "Bible and Plough" Program."[66]

On the whole, the suffering of West African women during this period in West African history is beyond human comprehension.

A Brief Look at the Role of Women in One West African Culture - The Akan – During the Introduction of Colonization and Christianization.

Africa once had over 2,000 languages with various different dialects; however, many of these languages have now died out. The same condition applied to West Africa and its different countries. As mentioned above, I have singled out the Gold Coast, in that part of the Guinea Coast which has been known as Ghana since independence from the British Empire in 1957, which is estimated to have had about forty-three languages. However, only a few are left now. Another reason for choosing Ghana is that the country has many slave-trading forts, which were built there and are still standing there today. These include the British Fort William at Anumabu, the British James Fort in the capital of Accra, the Danish-Norwegian Christiansborg Castle at Osu, just outside Accra, and the Portuguese Fort at Elmina or Edina, to mention just a few. Many of the slaves from the Guinea Coast area were shipped from the dungeons of these castles and forts in the Gold Coast, hence many women suffered badly in the dungeons as well as in the markets of these castles and forts.

Again, I have singled out Gold Coast partly because I should like to give a further brief account of the Akan ethnic group of people there, with their many dialects, who make up about 45% of present-day Ghana's population of nearly 25.37 million inhabitants. This means that 11.5 million are Akan, with their various dialects as well as their eight clans. These are: Aduana, Agona, Asakyiri, Asenie, Asona, Bretuo, Ekuona and Oyoko (2012 Ghana Census).

The Akan of Ghana, as already mentioned, originally migrated from the old well-developed great empire of Ghana in the Western Sudan, which flourished just south of the Sahara Desert during ancient times, to the Asante Region, in the western part of the Guinea Coast, before the Gold Coast came into existence(67). I have chosen this group of people because, although they resisted the patriarchal descent system which was brought by both the Muslims and the Christians, much of their cultural heritage under their matriarchal descent system was eventually destroyed anyway, negatively affecting their women forever.

A simple example of how some of the cultural heritage was destroyed, right from the 19th Century to this day, was a bitter complaint I heard from a lawyer I met once during my research work. She complained to me that, when she was born, as her parents were Akan from two different groups - one Asante and the other Akyem - she was first given her feminine soul name, which, according to the Akan, signifies the day of the week on which her soul arrived in this dimension on this Planet, Mother Earth. Then, when she was one week old, her second name followed, which was a very important ancestral family feminine name to preserve their family history.

However, as both her parents were Christians, they had to baptize her in a Christian Church. Then, the pastor had to drop her first name, which was her own soul name, as explained above. The pastor dropped this soul name in order to give her a female European Christian first name from the Holy Bible, as such African soul names were not given in the name of Jesus Christ, but were considered "devilish".

The second shock came when she started school. Again, her important ancestral feminine name, her second name, also had to be dropped in order to take her father's masculine surname in accordance with the customs of the European Christian Missionaries. Finally, her third shock came when she got married. Again, she had to drop her father's masculine surname in order to take her husband's foreign masculine surname, which was also her husband's father's masculine surname, in accordance with the rules of the foreign European Christian missionaries' patriarchal descent systems in their various countries.

In the end, according to this woman, this brought confusion around her. Her family and clan members and those people who had known her since she was born kept on calling her with her "soul" first name followed by her ancestral feminine name. In school she was known by her foreign Christian name and her father's masculine name. Then, later on, she was officially known by her European Christian feminine first name, followed by her foreigner-husband's, surname which was also this foreigner's father's surname. "Akosua" was the "soul" name of a female born on a Sunday, and "Serwaa" was an old Akan ancestral female name going back over two thousand years. Therefore this woman, to begin with, was called "Akosua Serwaa". When she was baptized, she became "Martha Serwaa". When she went to school, she became known as, "Martha Oben", as Oben was her father's surname. Then, when she married a foreigner called Mr. Smith, she became "Martha Smith". Therefore, she told me that, throughout her life, she has had four different names, that is, she had represented four different entities, depending on where she was, who she was with, and what she was doing.

This is just one example of confusion brought about in the lives of women in the Gold Coast, West Africa, through colonization and Christianization as the foreigners introduced their own culture. In the end, West African women were the losers.

The next confusion related to language. Many historians of West Africa state that there used to be about 43 languages on the Gold Coast up to the Northern Territories and the British part of Togoland. However, most of them have died out. The Akan language alone used to have about 23 dialects, most of which have died out. The Twi and Fante dialects are two of the few important Akan dialects that have survived in modern Ghana today. The English language was imposed in schools and offices and at official meetings.

Each language has its own culture and traditions; many languages of the Guinea Coast died out, together with their cultures and traditions, because they were ignored altogether by the colonialists and missionaries. This is partly because they used translators from where they settled. Therefore, the reading of the Holy Christian Bible in a language that only a few people could speak properly, or even in a dialect of the same language that others found it difficult to read due to literal translations, made it difficult for many West Africans to follow certain important points in the Holy Bible, as many people were not good enough at the English language to read it in English. This commotion caused many of the various languages and their dialects to die out.

More confusion arose from translations from the various Christian European languages into the various ethnic languages and their dialects. Most of the translations were not good enough as translations could not be done in all the dialects of the different languages; in the end, this meant that some parts of the Christian Holy Bible were sometimes seriously misunderstood. This brought confusion amongst the Akan women's traditional storytellers and singers, who wanted to tell or sing some verses of the Holy Bible in their Christian churches, and also tell some of these strange foreign stories to their people who could not read or write. In the end, women were the losers, as the colonialists and missionaries did not encourage women to have formal education to enable them to read the Christian Holy Bible in the foreign European missionaries' own languages.

Christianization upset other values in Akan culture. To begin with, the Akan had their own culture based on matriarchal descent system and maternal inheritance within their clan groups. The matrilineal system of inheritance was not only based on inheriting material wealth, but also on security, a kind of life insurance so that women never became destitute, as well as for clan purity.

Regarding purity, if a man and a woman from the same clan met and wanted to marry, they could not, even if they did not know each other and their families did not have any connection, or even if they lived in different parts of the country. This is because clan members were considered to be brothers and sisters from way back in ancient times, and therefore thought to have the same body chemistry. Therefore, such a sexual relationship would amount to incest and cause genetic problems for their children later on. However, when a man died leaving a wife and young children who needed fatherly care, any of his living brothers could be asked to marry the widow, in order to be a father to the young children that the brother had left behind. But both the widow and the brother-in-law had to agree, and the circumstances were favorable as the two were not from the same clan. This was to protect a woman from becoming destitute and helpless, with little children with no fatherly figure for their upbringing. Such relationships were therefore mainly for the children's sake. On the other hand, if the widow said no to the arrangement of a new marriage, then such a proposal could not be carried out.

Women had great respect in those ancient days, due to the fact that every human being came from a particular mother's womb, whereas any man could be declared the father of a child as there was no DNA test in those olden days. Even in modern times, when I was discussing some of these ancient cultures with some people one day, they asked me how many people nowadays go and have this test done in order to know their true biological fathers. They argued, "Only mothers know!"

In Akan culture, the older women became, the more powerful they became and therefore more respect was shown to them. This contrasts with Western Christian civilization, in which women hide their ages since men do not respect old women. But these Akan women became more powerful and wiser, and therefore became the head of their families, extended families or clans, side by side with the old men, who were another type of family head complementary to the old women's power and responsibilities. In families and clans of ancient times, the old woman - called "Nana" in Twi, or "Nananom" in the plural - would sometimes have been behind the scenes during certain meetings; however, they still had the power to veto any decisions taken at such meetings attended by only the men which they did not agree to. Unfortunately, the chattel slave trade, colonization and Christianization destroyed these Akan women's veto power forever.

I have fully researched Akan oral history, including poems and songs as well as a few recorded by ancient West African foreign travelers. According to these records, before Christianity was introduced, the Akan clan women knew their history and folktales very well, and told them to the young. Some of the women were also priestesses, spiritual or psychic healers and herbal medicine women, who the British called "witch doctors". One of their special duties was that, whenever there was a war and some of their people went to the battlefield, these female "witch doctors" performed special rituals, appealing to God the Creator, through the ancestral spirits and the lesser goddesses and gods, for the soldiers' safety and success. If some did not return, the women in these clans helped to organize the affairs of their families. All these Akan women's traditions disappeared when colonialism and Christianity were introduced after the chattel slave trade.

On the other hand, in Akan culture, just as men respected women, women were brought up also to have great respect for men as physical protectors and as providers of food and other necessities in life. There were certain activities that a woman was not expected to do, and there were certain abusive words a woman could not say to a man. Also, to be able to attend certain special meetings, a woman had to have the company of a man, and vice versa, that is, there were certain meetings where a man had to have the company of a woman in order to attend.

There was a customary delegation of duties between these Akan women and their men. For example, the men were responsible for clearing the forests, cutting down heavy trees, and getting the fields ready for the women to plant and sow the seeds. Before farming work started, people always prayed to the female farming goddess, "Asase Yaa", for her protection from accidents such as wounds, drowning, poisonous snake bites, wild animal attacks, and so on.

The Akan women also washed gold along the rivers sometimes; this depended on where they lived, as some of the Akan groups of people, like the Akyem, lived in areas where most of the rivers were full of gold nuggets. The men who were interested in the gold industry took more active roles in deep-pit gold digging. The men also hunted and did large-scale group fishing, "kwagyan", to provide meat and fish. Women, meanwhile, were very active in a special type of fishing which was also done in groups. They also sold some of their products for financial support for their families, besides being great traders of various kinds of merchandise.

Again, according to the traditional Akan oral history which I researched fully, when the Akan moved to the forest region of the Guinea Coast, the Akan women were just as active as their men in making all sorts of artifacts. These women were very good at making pottery and beads. They made special cloth, sponges and dyes from special tropical forest trees. The Akan men were also engaged in the making of leather to be sold to the Arab traders. They made wooden sandals, as well as beautiful leather sandals which were worn by queens, kings, chiefs and other aristocrats on special occasions. On the whole, people walked about barefoot or sometimes used wooden sandals on special occasions. The men also wove beautiful, colorful clothing known as "Kente", worn on special occasions by queens, kings and aristocrats, and metal and gold artifacts and jewelry for special ceremonial days. These men were also very good wood carvers: they did carpentry work, built houses and primitive footpaths, and undertook all the heavy and dangerous work, as well as going into battle to protect their people. The Akan women also took part in some battles, as explained in part one of this book. In the end, however, the colonization and Christianization processes in the Guinea Coast area, which were introduced in the wrong way by the Europeans who ignored Akan women's position in their culture, as well as their complementary existence with their men, created chaotic relationship between women and men.

In home matters, Akan women dominated, as mentioned in part one of this book. Under normal circumstances, men were not allowed in the kitchens or to make food, as the women decided many matters concerning the daily running of their homes. In the same way, women were not expected to perform certain hard work which was performed only by men. Therefore, you can understand how Akan women needed their men, and the men needed their women too. This culture resulted in complementary existence. This tradition was completely destroyed by the introduction of colonialism and Christianity, based on a culture of patriarchal descent system, which was brought to West Africa by these Christian European colonialists and their missionaries.

There was another way in which European Christian missionaries did not show respect for the local women who were members of their churches, according to some oral historians that I met during my travels in West Africa. An important point here is that the European writers were not interested in native women's affairs. Therefore, certain important information about many things that affected women were never recorded.

One example was that, in the early days of Christianity in the Gold Coast, in the late 19th and early 20th Centuries, women and men could not sit together in church. The European Christian missionaries made sure that men always sat in comfort, in the part of the church reserved for men, in order that they could pay proper attention to the words of Jesus Christ. Meanwhile, women with babies, little children, boys and girls, sat in another part of the church, where there was always a commotion. To the missionaries, it did not matter much whether the women heard the words of God or not. Since the women were being ordered to listen to their men in everything, the presence of these women was enough for the pastor or priest.

In addition to this segregation, all the Christian women had to cover their hair. Women with short cut beautiful queen-mothers style haircuts or beautifully plaited hairstyles had to cover their heads with scarves in the church. One interesting modern example of the continuation of this old Christian missionary tradition from the 19th Century is that, as late as the 1940s, many old women remember that teenage schoolgirls in some towns in the Gold Coast were not allowed to attend certain Christian church services without covering completely their simple haircuts or plaited hair. To complicate matters, in some Christian churches, schoolgirls had to put on European dresses to go to church, as traditional clothes were not allowed. One old woman said that once, as a frustrated young schoolgirl, she was sent out of a church service to go home and put on her European dress and a scarf for her hair. She sighed and said, "May Jesus Christ have mercy on us African women."

In the next chapter, there are a few unusual arguments - one ancient, the others, modern - regarding the importance of the women's welfare in our human existence, that these Christian European colonialists and missionaries were not aware of or deliberately chose to ignore.

Picture 16: The Asante Queen Mother At A Ceremony In Kumase The Capital Of The Asante Kingdom

CHAPTER 14

RECOMMENDED SPECIAL ATTENTION FOR FEMALES

a. An Ancient Legend
b. The Philosopher/Educationalist
c. The Village Women and Girls
d. The Medical Professor/Scientist
e. A Brief Summary of Women's Position in Some West African Cultures after the Migration

In connection with the unfortunate way that Christian European colonization, as well as their wrong way of introducing Christianity, which destroyed West African women's traditional lives forever, I should like to present here a few impartial intellectual arguments regarding the special care and attention to be given to females because of their roles as foundational cornerstones of human existence on this planet.

a. An Ancient Legend

I will begin with an ancient Egyptian legend telling us of a woman's role in her society. This legend can be found in one of the oldest records of Ancient Egypt, which dates back to 163 BC(68). The legend is as follows: a young girl, who had been brought up in one of the temples in ancient Egypt, had been begging for money for some time, to save up for her marriage dowry. Her savings had been given to one of the men in the temple for safekeeping. Now that she had reached puberty, and had to go through some puberty rites to prepare for her marriage, she needed the money back. These rites included a pact with God, to be sealed with the circumcision of her clitoris: a tiny mark would be made at the top of her clitoris with a sharp knife, in order to let some blood come out. This mark, made on a very precious part of her physical body, was a symbol to promise God that, now that she had reached adulthood and would marry and have children, she would be the family's foundational cornerstone as a mother and wife, and would always stand firm for the family, no matter what happened.

This offers food for thought regarding a woman's responsibilities in this world. A female has to be psychologically strong to see to it that her family and clan affairs are getting on reasonably well, and are in harmony with the society in which they live in. Such are the responsibilities of "cornerstones", the foundation on which solid families, clans and societies are built.

b. The Philosopher/Educationalist

The second argument for the importance of a woman's position in her society is as follows. The famous Ghanaian educationalist and philosopher, Dr. James Emmanuel Kwegyir Aggrey (1875-1927), born at Anamabu, Gold Coast, once said:

> “Educate a man and you educate an individual; but educate a woman and you educate a nation”.

He said this because, as has been already discussed, in the early colonial days in the Gold Coast, many girls were not sent to school, as the Christian European missionaries were not keen on educating females. Their main argument was that, whatever a woman's education, she would end up in the kitchen, whereas a man had to use his education to make all the important decisions for the family, as well as to work to support his family. This was the European Christian Missionaries' policy, with which this famous philosopher disagreed.

As already discussed, in the old days in Christian Europe, the men treated their women as second-class citizens, as was their culture. To this day, even though women in the Western world have struggled for more than a century and have achieved some degree of equality with their men, these women are still struggling for a more equal status in all walks of life.

Therefore, as stated elsewhere in this book, when the European Christian missionaries brought formal education to West Africa, they did not encourage formal education for females, due to their own patriarchal cultural background. Therefore, the colonialism and Christian missionary work which followed the chattel slave trade did not encourage equality between men and women. Consequently, their own European women, from the early 20th Century to this day, have had to fight for the emancipation of women. In the same way, to this day in West Africa, where women's lives have badly been affected, they have to follow the Western women's example and fight for the emancipation of African women too[(69)].

c. The Village Women and Girls

The next story about the importance of females' position in their societies is as follows. Once, in early 1992 when I was doing more anthropological fieldwork in Ghana, I came across a group of girls and women in one of the Akan villages in the Asante region. They were preparing for the performance of "puberty rites" for a young schoolgirl who had just had her first menstruation, and therefore had to go through this rite to prepare her to marry later on when she finished her education.

In the old days, such puberty rites acted as a kind of life insurance for a woman. Any woman who had gone through this initiation was considered a natural cornerstone for her family, clan and society, and would never be destitute whether she was able to have children or not. Also, in case of illness or economic hardship, or in her old age when she became helpless, her family, her extended family, her clan or her society as a whole would come to her aid and take good care of her until she died. Therefore the celebration of puberty rites was very important. Unlike in modern times; when Christian teenage girls are confirmed in their various Christian religions, who cares what happens to them later on in life? The only insurance for them is that, in case of death, their Christian religious leaders at where they lived would bury them, on condition that they had been paying their church dues until their death.

To return to the Akan village girls preparing to celebrate the puberty rite of the young teenager: to begin with, unlike the ancient girl preparing for her puberty rite somewhere in ancient Egypt, the Akan never practiced female circumcision. They also had no tradition of tribal body markings, unlike some other West African tribes, although they did have a tradition of body decoration with special red or white clay, for special occasions. Therefore, during the celebration of this Akan teenager's puberty rites, there was no cutting of tribal markings and no circumcision, but only special ritual performance and a little body decoration with special clay.

On the other hand, in certain circumstances some individual Akan, as already mentioned in this book, may have a few special tribal markings made for personal reasons. For example, such marks made with a knife could cure or protect against convulsion and other special diseases, or could fulfil other special personal serious needs, including spiritual matters. Otherwise, as the expression of such a taboo goes in the Twi dialect of the Akan language, "Yekyiri Sekan"; that means that marking our skins with knives is forbidden, and this goes back to ancient times[70].

When I came across these girls and women who were very busy and excited preparing for this celebration of puberty rites, I unwittingly provoked these girls and women by asking why their culture does not have special rites for teenage boys too. I was once told, a long time ago, that their teenage boys used to have some special "training" in ancient times corresponding to the girls' puberty celebrations, but I did not tell them this. Then I continued, telling them that in some African cultures, they still have special ceremonies for teenage boys. One schoolgirl, somewhere in the background, shouted at me that the purpose of the boys' ceremonies was to teach them how to go to war and kill human beings, as well as how to make fun of women in bed to make them pregnant. She continued to say, at top of her voice, that such male ceremonies had nothing to do with teaching these boys how to take good care of their homes for their children and wives, nor how to offer help for their families and to anybody else who might need their help, one way or another, in their society.

This girl surprised me. I did not want to defend the boys even though two of my own children are males.

Then our discussion continued. A woman, the group argued, is very important for the continuation of the human species. Imagine a young man having to bear a living thing in his stomach for up to nine months: a living thing that sometimes kicks, moves, and also makes the bearer sick, depressed, and tired, or makes him vomit. How could a man, even with all his physical strength, withstand these conditions?

Again, another girl continued saying, that when the baby is born, it needs very gentle care, patience and love, as well as natural food - that is, breast-milk - to help this newly-arrived and helpless being to survive. They asked me as to how a man could have the psychological strength and patience to go through all this. They also added that, for these reasons, God is not stupid to put a woman in charge of pregnancy, as well as of children and family care. Hence, women are created very special, therefore men are always jealous of women.

This conversation slowly turned into a philosophical discussion in which they continued to argue that women were created weak on purpose to suit their mission on this planet, which is very important. However, a man's responsibilities to family life are just as important in their way, but different and therefore complementary. A man must see to it that the family has sufficient food, clothing and shelter and other necessities, which entails hard work, physically and otherwise.

These women and girls also argued that this philosophy of men and women's complementary roles in the culture of the Akan ethnic group of Ghana, in which there is great respect for both women and men through the delegation of duties, was not encouraged by the Western Christian culture brought to West Africa. They also argued that the white man puts the white woman in the secondary place, despite her great spiritual responsibilities.

In the end, I held my peace and left quickly amid wild shouts of, "Goodbye, Mama! Are you coming to join us later? There will be plenty food, drumming and dancing!"

Thus, my short encounter with these women and girls, some of them were completely illiterate, gave me food for thought regarding African women's positions, even in our modern society.

Picture 17: Akan Teenage Girl Going Through The Akan Puberty Rights Ceremony

d. The Medical Professor/Scientist

In continuation of the above discussions, I was amazed to read articles that appeared in the BBC World Service program not long ago. According to this report[71], a medical doctor, professor and researcher (MD, FRS, CBE) based in London, UK, has written research articles entitled:

> **"BIRTHWEIGHT'S LINK TO LIFE-LONG HEALTH"**
>
> **"NINE MONTHS THAT MADE YOU"**
>
> **"PREVENTION OF CHRONIC DISEASES DEPENDS LARGELY ON THE IMPROVEMENT IN THE NUTRITION OF GIRLS AND YOUNG WOMEN"**

In his argument, this professor says research has proved that famine can affect babies' brains so that, for example, babies' brains age faster. Also, baby famine can also cause schizophrenia. The Professor's main argument is as follows:

> "Our early development in the womb sets up our constitution, how vulnerable we are to negative things that we encounter and how we will cope with them for the rest of our lives."

He therefore recommended that special care should be taken in the upbringing and the development of girls growing up.

This professor's scientific research results are more or less in line with the arguments of the philosopher/educationalist, the village women and girls, and the ancient Egyptian teenager's future responsibilities as a woman.

All these opinions are completely different from the opinions of many cultures about women's responsibilities in this world, including the opinions of those Christian European chattel slave traders, colonialists and missionaries.

e. A Brief Summary of Women's Position in Some West African Cultures after the Migration

Below is a summary of those four separate arguments and their information about the importance of human female's responsibilities for the safe existence of humanity on this planet. These are:

1. The girl preparing to have a pact with God in Egypt in order to be a cornerstone for her family
2. The philosopher and educationalist talking about the importance of women's formal education
3. The women and girls preparing for puberty rites, where the teenager is prepared to assume responsibilities as a foundation cornerstone for her family and her Akan clan later on
4. The interesting scientific evidence of the importance of a woman's contribution to our human species, hence the great care that is needed to protect young females from various health hazards

These arguments clearly point to the roles of women as foundation cornerstones of human existence on this planet Earth. Therefore, any condition that could upset women's role in society could bring about irreparable damage to their societies and to the human species. This ignorance, unfortunately, did happen in the Gold Coast, on West Africa's Guinea Coast, which became Ghana when the country attained her independence from the Christian British colonial masters in 1957. After the end of their chattel slave trading, which lasted for nearly 400 years. They continued the damage through their colonization and Christian mission work, ultimately destroying forever the important roles of the Gold Coast women's heritage. To this day, the forts and castles built by these foreigners still stand as everlasting monuments for the dark ages for women in the Guinea Coast.

Although slavery previously existed all over the world, including in Europe as well as in many cultures on the Guinea Coast, these practices, in which slaves became their owners' kin, were not as brutal or beastly as the chattel slave trading. In this trade, slaves became "commodities" or "things", like animals which could be disposed of anyhow, anywhere, and were also shipped away to many remote places in the Northern Hemisphere. Besides, these chattel slaves were treated as animals in dungeons underneath their masters' castles and forts along the Guinea Coast, and were also treated as "cargo" in the dungeons of the European Christians' ships. Previously in the Akan culture, for example, slaves captured on the battlefield or to settle debts were immediately absorbed into their masters' families; slaves therefore had kin straight away and belonged to specific societies.

CHAPTER 15

THE CHRISTIAN EUROPEAN CHATTEL SLAVE-TRADING CASTLES AND FORTS BUILT ON THE GUINEA COAST (GOLD COAST, NOW GHANA)

The following is the concrete, lasting evidence in Ghana now of how Christian Europe came all the way to the Guinea Coast, with their guns and alcoholic drinks in one hand and the Christian Holy Bible in the other, to confuse and trick the natives who were mistaken for not knowing anything about the Almighty God, the Creator. This mistake has wounded generations of West Africans, especially West African women and their prestigious positions in their societies, forever. This irreparable mistake was made by Christian Europe.

a. The Chattel Slave-Trading Forts and Posts Built by the Brandenburgers (now one of the Sixteen Federal States of Germany. Its Capital is Potsdam)

1. Dorothea at Akwida, built by the Brandenburgers in 1685, was besieged and taken by the local people in 1690. However, it was restored in 1698, and then abandoned about 1709.
2. A small fort was built at Takrama in 1694, but was abandoned in 1708 or 1709.
3. The Brandenburgers built the castle Gross Friedrichsburg, situated between Axim and Cape Three Points built in 1685. This castle was

abandoned, together with all their other possessions, in 1708 or 1709. Since then, the castle was occupied on and off by the local chieftain until 1725, when the Dutch occupied this Castle in order to prevent others taking it over. However, the Dutch did not use it for anything.

b. The British Chattel Slave-Trading Castles and Forts Built on the Guinea Coast

1. James Fort, Accra, built by the English in 1673.
2. Vernon at Prampram, built about 1787.
3. Christiansborg Castle, Osu, near Accra, bought from the Danes by the British in 1850.
4. Prinzenstein at Keta, bought from the Danes in 1850.
5. Konigstein at Ada, bought from the Danes in 1850.
6. Friedenborg at Ningo, bought from the Danes in 1850.
7. Augustaborg at Teshi, bought from the Danes in 1850.
8. Crevecoeur at Accra was built by the Dutch, but they ceded it to the British in 1867, who renamed it Ussher Fort.
9. The English built a fort at Shido in the seventeenth century, but it was abandoned before 1700.
10. A Dutch fort, built at Beraku in 1667, was taken over by the British in 1782.
11. The British fort at Winneba, built in the seventeenth century, was abandoned in 1813 but reoccupied two years later.
12. Fort Leydsamheid at Apam, constructed by the Dutch in 1697, was renamed Fort Patience when it

was taken over by the British in 1782.

13. Fort Tantamkweri was built by the British before 1726, but they abandoned it in 1820.
14. The spectacularly situated Castle Amsterdam, at Kormantine, was built by the English in 1631. After a series of take overs, including by the Dutch and the Asante, it was finally ceded to the British in 1867.
15. A fortified lodge" was built at Egya by the English in 1663; it was taken over by the Dutch, but was retaken in 1664.
16. Fort William at Anomabu, built by the English sometime after 1673, possibly during the reign of William III.
17. A small lodge was built at Anashan by the English about 1660, and taken over by the Dutch in 1665.
18. A small post, Nassau, built at Mori by the Dutch in 1598, who extended it to a Castle in 1624. After a lot of takeovers, it was finally ceded to the British in 1867.
19. Fort Royal, built at Amanfur by the Danes in 1658, was bought by the English in 1685.
20. Cape Coast Castle was built by the Swedes in 1652, but after many complicated takeovers by others, was retaken by the English in 1664.
21. St. George Fort at Elmina, after many takeovers by other Europeans, was bought by the British in 1872.
22. Vredenburg Fort at Kommenda was built by the Dutch in 1688. After an attack by local people, the British took it over and destroyed it in 1782.
23. A fort was built at Kommenda in 1670 by the English

and later abandoned. It was rebuilt in 1695, but was ceded to the Dutch in 1867.

24. Fort St. Sebastian at Shama was built by the Portuguese, but after several takeovers by others, it was bought by the British in 1872.
25. Fort Orange at Sekondi was built by the Dutch in 1670. After many disputes the local Ahanta people destroyed it in 1694, and the British bought it in 1872.
26. Another fort was built by the English at Sekondi about 1680. After many takeovers and disputes with other Europeans and with local people, the British bought it back in 1872.
27. Castle Batenstein at Butri was built by the Dutch in 1598 and 1640. However, after the usual problems in those days, it was eventually sold to the British in 1872.
28. Fort Metal Cross was built at Dixcove by the English in 1691. However, after many problems with the local people, it was ceded to the Dutch in 1867, but the British bought it back in 1872.
29. Fort Apollonia at Beyin, built by the British in 1750, was ceded to the Dutch in 1867 and then abandoned.
30. Fort St. Anthony at Axim was built by the Portuguese and was renovated and enlarged in 1515. After many disputes with other European traders, was finally bought by the British in 1872

c. The Danish-Norwegian Kingdom Chattel Slave-Trading Castles and Forts Built on the Guinea Coast

1. Fort Prinzenstein at Keta was built by the Danes in 1784. After some problems with the local people, it was sold to the British in 1850.

2. Fort Konigstein at Ada was built by the Danes in 1784, and sold to the British in 1850.

3. Fort Friedenborg at Ningo was built by the Danes in 1734, and sold to the British in 1850.

4. Fort Augustaborg at Teshi was built by the Danes in 1787, and sold to the British in 1850.

5. Christiansborg Castle at Osu, just outside Accra, was just a trading post for the Portuguese from 1578, after their small trading post in Accra was destroyed by the local people in 1645. However, it was rebuilt as a castle by the Swedes in 1657, and then taken over by the Danes in 1659. The Danes sold it to the Portuguese in 1679, but bought it back three years later. But then in 1693, a native man called Asameni and his people from Akwamu occupied this castle. However, they sold it back to the Danes in the following year. In 1850, the Danes sold Christiansborg Castle to the British(72).

6. Fort William at Anomabu was originally built by the English sometime after 1673. But there was previously a Swedish fort in this town, which was taken and destroyed by the Danes in 1659, but was besieged later on by the Ashanti in 1807.

7. Fort Royal at Amanfur was built by the Danes in 1658, but sold to the English in 1685.

8. Cape Coast Castle, built at Cape Coast by the Swedes in 1652, was taken by the Danes in 1659, and was subsequently taken over several times by the natives and the various other European slave traders.

9. Fort Witsen at Takoradi was built by the Swedes about 1652, possibly on the site of an old French post. The Danes took it over in 1657, and then it was taken over by various European traders, and finally

destroyed and abandoned by the Dutch. Later on, a smaller building was built on the site.

d. The Dutch Chattel Slave-Trading Castles and Forts Built on the Guinea Coast

1. Fort Crevecoeur at Accra was built by the Dutch in 1650. After many takeovers and abandonments, it was ceded to the British in 1867, and renamed Ussher Fort.

2. A fort at Beraku was built by the Dutch in 1667; it was taken over by the British in 1782, but given back to the Dutch who abandoned it later on.

3. Fort Leydsamheid at Apam was given the name Fort Patience by the local people, who seriously opposed its construction in 1697. Due to their resistance, the Dutch builders could not finish this building until 1702. The British took it over in 1782 and restored it in 1785, but it was destroyed by Atta Wusu from the Akan State of Akim in 1811.

4. The spectacularly situated Amsterdam Castle at Kormantine, built by the English in 1631, was taken by the Dutch under de Ruyter in 1665. After another take-over by Captain Shirley, R.N., in 1782, it was restored to the Dutch three years later. However, the Asante occupied it in 1807; it was later occupied again by the Dutch, and finally ceded to the British in 1867.

5. A small house, like a fortified small lodge, was built at Egya by the English in 1663. It was taken over by the Dutch, but was retaken by the Englishman Captain Robert Holms in 1664.

6. Another small lodge, built at Anashan by the English in 1660, was taken by the Dutch in 1665, but later abandoned.

7. Nassau was a small slave trading post built at Mori in 1598 by the Dutch, who later built a Castle there. This was taken by the Englishman Captain Holmes in 1664. It was retaken by the Dutch Admiral de Ruyter in 1665, retaken by the British in 1782, ceded to the Dutch in 1785, and, finally, ceded to the British in 1867.

8. A small fort at Queen Anne's Point, near Cape Coast, was built by the Dutch, but was abandoned before 1662.

9. Cape Coast Castle, originally built by the Swedes in 1652, was taken by the Danes in 1659, then by the local people, the Fetu, in 1660. In 1661 it was once more taken by the Dutch; in 1662, by the English; by the Dutch in 1663; and the English in 1664. It was then held against the Dutch the following year.

10. St. George Fort at Elmina was built by the Portuguese in 1482 and taken by the Dutch in 1637. It was greatly strengthened and was provided with satellite redoubts, and then sold to the British in 1872.

11. Fort Vredenburg at Kommenda was built by the Dutch in 1688. The Kommenda people tried to occupy it seven years later, but did not succeed. The British took it over and destroyed it in 1782.

12. The English built a fort at Kommenda in 1670. It was abandoned, but rebuilt in 1695. It was ceded to the Dutch in 1867, and later abandoned.

13. Fort St. Sebastian at Shama was built by the Portuguese. It was taken and enlarged by the Dutch in 1640. In 1664 it was taken by the English Captain Holmes, then it was retaken by the Dutch Admiral de Ruyter in 1665. It was sold to the British in 1872.

14. Fort Orange at Sekondi was built by the Dutch about 1670. It was taken and destroyed by the Ahanta, the local people, in 1694. But the Dutch rebuilt it and it was finally sold to the British in 1872.
15. A fort at Sekondi, built in 1680 by the English, was also taken and destroyed by the Ahanta in 1698. Later on the English rebuilt it, but it was taken by the French in 1779. In 1867, it was ceded to the Dutch, but then in 1872, the British bought it back.
16. Fort Witsen at Takoradi was built by the Swedes about 1652, probably on the site of old French trading post. This fort was taken by the Danes in 1657, but the Dutch took it over soon afterwards. The English Captain Holmes captured it in 1664, then the Dutch Admiral de Ruyter took it in 1665, then it was destroyed and abandoned. However, the Dutch subsequently reoccupied it again and built a smaller fort.
17. Post Batenstein at Butri was built by the Dutch in 1598, and they built a castle there in 1640. After many disputes in 1664 and 1665, the British bought it in 1872.
18. Fort Metal Cross at Dixcove was built by the English in 1691. After attacks and disputes with local traders, it was ceded to the Dutch in 1867, but it was bought back by the British in 1872.
19. Fort Apollonia at Beyin was built by the British in 1750, but ceded to the Dutch in 1867, and then abandoned.
20. Castle Gross Friedrichsburg, between Axim and Cape Three Points, was built by the Brandenburgers in 1685. This Fort was abandoned together with the rest of their possessions in 1708 or 1709. But the local

chieftain intermittently occupied it from the time of its abandonment until 1725, when the Dutch occupied it to protect it from other rivals, even though the place was never of great use for them.

21. Fort St. Anthony at Axim was built by the Portuguese during the early days of their arrival. In 1515, it was very much enlarged and fortified. It was their last Fort, but was taken by the Dutch in 1642. In 1664, the English Captain Holmes took it, but then the Dutch Admiral de Ruyter took it back in 1665. Finally, the British bought it in 1872.

22. Fort Duma on the river Ankobra, which was built by the Portuguese in 1623, was destroyed by an earthquake in 1636. Later on the Dutch took it during their occupation of the other Portuguese possessions, but it was later abandoned.

23. Fort Ruyghaver on river Ankobra was built by the Dutch about 1640. However, it was taken by the local people in 1680.

24. Fort Carthago, also on river Ankobra, was also built by the Dutch about 1640. It was soon abandoned.

e. The French Chattel Slave-Trading Castles and Forts Built on the Guinea Coast

1. There was a small French trading post at Kommenda, which was taken and destroyed by the local people in 1688.

2. A fort at Sekondi was built by the English in 1680, but was taken by the local Ahanta people in 1698. Four years later, the English took it back and rebuilt it. But, this time, it was taken by the French w in 1779. It was then ceded to the Dutch in 1867, but then the British

bought it in 1872.

3. Fort Witsen at Takoradi, built by the Swedes in 1652, might have been built on the site of an old French post. The records are not clear.

f. The Swedish Chattel Slave-Trading Castles and Forts Built on the Guinea Coast

1. The site of Christiansborg Castle might have been occupied by the Portuguese from 1578 to 1645. However, the Castle was built by the Swedes in 1657 and taken by the Danes in 1659.
2. There was a Swedish fort at Anomabu, but it was taken and destroyed by the Danes in 1659. It was besieged by the Asante in 1807.
3. Cape Coast Castle, built by the Swedes in 1652, was taken by the Danes in 1659. It was then taken by the local Fetu people in 1660. The Dutch took it in 1661, then the English took it in 1662. The Dutch took it again in 1663, but then the English Captain Holmes took it from the Dutch Admiral de Ruyter in the following year.
4. Fort Witsen at Takoradi was built by the Swedes about 1652, possibly on the site of an old French post. The fort was taken by the Danes in 1657. Soon afterwards, the Dutch took it, then the English took it in 1664, then the Dutch also took it in 1665 before destroying and abandoning it. However, the site was used later on for a smaller building.

Picture 18: One Of The Chattel Slave Traders' Castles: The Famous Cape Coast Castle Built By The Swedes In 1652

CONCLUSION

The full account of the most prestigious positions occupied by ancient West African women when their tribes migrated from the Nile Valley regions to the Western Sudan, as well as the most extraordinary deadly downfall they suffered later on, are beyond human comprehension. Therefore, such a full account is also beyond the scope of this work.

I have given the nickname "TOPPLED CORNERSTONES", to those ancient West African women, who first bore great responsibilities as God's own foundation stones for their societies' development, but were later toppled and destroyed by male foreigners. Women, these foundation cornerstones who are the physical channels for human beings to come into existence on this Planet Earth, have been misunderstood and therefore mishandled in many ways. A full debate about this subject is beyond the scope of this work. Hence, a full account of the women's lives in the Western Sudan in ancient West Africa is also beyond the scope of this book. Therefore, in this work, I have given only a summary of these women's rise and their tragic fall when they came into contact with people from foreign cultures where women were treated differently.

As mentioned in the Introduction, that part of West Africa called the Western Sudan is in many ways one of the most extraordinarily beautiful and unique regions of the African Continent. The area is full of lakes, rivers and streams, as well as mountains and hills. It stretches from the savannah, from the fringes of the Sahara Desert, the largest and the most spectacular desert on this planet, and then down southwards to the Guinea Coast and the shores of the Atlantic Ocean. The area was also full of a great variety of vegetation, as well as abundance of natural mineral resources including gold and diamonds. On top of all these, there is also the most extraordinary collection of birds and animal species belonging to the various animal kingdoms. The area is also the famous route for seasonal migration of special birds from Northern Europe to Africa.

Both the Arab Muslim traders and the Christian European chattel slave traders named this area the Western Sudan. Some of the numerous peoples belonging to the empires, kingdoms, nations and states who lived there included the tribes of Benin, Dahomey, Dogon, Hausa, Igbo-Ukwu, Kanem-Bornu, Mali, Mane, Mossi, Nok, Segu, Songhay, Wolof, and Yoruba, as well as the kingdom of the Akan, which belonged to the powerful Ghana Empire which was one of the biggest in that area.

However, tragically, what happened to women's affairs in the Western Sudan, from the West Africans' migration there from the Nile Valley until today, is beyond human comprehension, just like a fairytale. Therefore, in Part 1 of this work, I have given only a short summary of the origins of these West African kingdoms and empires from the Nile Valley region, close to Egypt, and how some of them migrated westwards. I have also given a short account of some interesting, unique accounts of women's responsibilities in those days in their societies.

This work also offers a brief account, in Parts 2 and 3, of Akan women's downfall through chattel slave trading, colonization and Christianization. These processes were conducted by Christian Europe when the Akan, with their numerous clans and dialects, migrated again to escape the influence of the Arab Muslims' invasion. This time, they migrated from the ancient powerful "Gana" (Ghana) Empire where they had settled, and went southwards towards the Guinea Coast of the Atlantic Ocean.

As I have explained, I have singled out this Akan ethnic group for two important reasons. First, the Akan clans were among the numerous migrants who left the Nile Valley Regions to come to West Africa. This tribe was therefore one of the kingdoms who came to settled in the powerful Ghana Empire. This Akan Kingdom migrated southwards again when the Arab Muslim merchants arrived in the northern part of West Africa's Sahara Desert to trade, buy slaves and spread their Muslim religion, as well as their patriarchal descent family system. This was at a time when these Muslims were leaving slowly southwards from their occupation of the Iberian Peninsula, an area which included Spain.

These Akan clans left just as the Muslims were arriving, causing cultures in the various empires and kingdoms across north-western Africa to break down. This was due to the introduction of Islam and its patriarchal descent system. This new religion seriously affected the cultures around based on matriarchal descent systems, in which women were cornerstones for their tribes and families. Therefore, although many of these tribes remained and accepted the Islamic religion, many other tribes decided to move southwards beyond the Savannah. Therefore, as the Akan did not want to become Muslims and lose their ancient heritage of matriarchal descent system, their religion and their entire cultural heritage, they also moved southwards from the Ghana Empire, to the Guinea Coast.

My second reason for choosing the Akan ethnic group is that, unfortunately for them, sometime after their arrival on the Guinea Coast, they met much more serious catastrophes, more serious than the occupation of the Arab Muslim traders and Islam. This time the new various catastrophic encounters were Christian Europe's chattel slave trading, colonization and Christianization.

Unfortunately, these new challenges destroyed the cultural heritage of the Akan tribe's women forever. Although one of the Akan groups, the Asante, confronted the colonialists of the Christian British Empire in two wars, the Asante lost. In the end, sadly enough, these proud, well-functioning Akan and the other Guinea Coast native ethnic groups ended up as colonial subjects of the Christian British Empire. These subjects of the British Empire had to take instructions from London after the deadly chattel slave trading.

The saddest part of this tragedy, was the permanent destruction of West African women's heritage of matriarchal descent, which made women foundation cornerstones for their families, clans and societies as a whole. The delegation of duties between women and men and the complementary existence between these two genders were destroyed forever, as many West African societies adopted patriarchal family descent systems.

During this era of changes, first, some of these women together with their men were sold as "commodities". Second, those women left behind lost forever their complementary relationship with their men, the delegation of duties between women and men, and their mutual respect for each other. Third, those women who were left behind were forced to copy in many ways the lifestyle of white Christian women in Europe, which was not suitable for West African women's way of life. This made these West African women lose many positive things in their cultural lifestyles.

On the whole, these phenomena - Christian Europe's chattel slave trading on Guinea Coast, followed by colonization, which was in turn followed by their wrong way of introducing their Christian religion through mission work - made the Gold Coast women lose their former outstanding status in their societies. They therefore left devastation and an everlasting deep scar on the lives of these West African women. But the saddest and the strangest point about this deep scar on the human heart is twofold.

First, to begin with, all the different religious leaders of Christian Europe - popes, bishops, pastors, and priests, all using the same Christian Holy Bible about Jesus Christ's message to humanity - backed this horrific treatment of West Africans, especially West African women.

Second, these West African Women were also let down by the fact that Christian Europe's ruling kings and queens did not see anything wrong with this type of slavery until much later on. Thus it was not until this North Atlantic chattel slavery had already been used as the foundation for Christian Europe's Industrial Revolution and its excessive material wealth (as argued by the retired schoolteacher above) that it was officially abolished: first by the Danes, followed by the British in 1807, and then the French and Americans a few years later.

However, the trade continued, unofficially and discretely, until nearly the end of the 19th Century. Another sad fact was that 24% of these chattel slaves in some parts of the New World, for example, in some Caribbean countries, were owned by European Christian women settlers. They were sometimes very brutal to their slave women, showing no solidarity with West African women(73).

In the end, in some West African tribes, the positive matriarchal descent system continued officially on the surface, yet it failed these West African women in many ways. The coastal West African women lost the status they had enjoyed since ancient times in terms of respect, good positions and equality with men, where men respected every woman irrespective of her position in society.

In those days, women were not looked upon as "sex objects". Men showed extraordinary great respect for women's roles as mothers, great war leaders and warriors, spiritual healers, herbal medicine healers, cultural custodians, great advisors in times of need, commercial leaders, and teachers. Women had social, constitutional, political and religious rights. All this was for the simple reason that all men on this planet, great or humble, came from a woman's womb, even those who were subsequently adopted by another woman, abandoned somewhere or raised in an orphanage. In the philosophies of the destroyed matriarchal descent system, which was the foundation cornerstone of all family structures, inheritance rights, appointment of kings, chiefs, other high-status clan and community appointments, names and titles given, all were based on a person's mother's status.

Some scholars have argued that this down-grading of West African women was not necessarily due to the foreign religious philosophies of Islam, Christianity and colonialism in themselves. Rather, it was because women back home in Europe, from where these foreigners came, were considered second-class human beings. In those cultures, even before these two religions were introduced, women's lives were characterized by sexual abuse and exploitation, drudgery, subservience, dependence, oppression and the exploitation of women's labor through polygamous marriages, or make-belief monogamous marriages[(74)]. All this took place under their patriarchal descend family systems, in their original religions and civilization, even before the two great religions of Christianity and Islam came into being in their countries.

It is important to note that, as already mentioned, slavery was a part of human nature and went on throughout the whole world, including both Europe and Africa. This was due to tribal wars, internal clan disputes or the scramble for territories, or was used as a way to settle disputes or debts. However, while victims remained in or near their masters' environments, some were absorbed into their captors' families, as was the case in the Akan clans. Also, in some of these ancient worldwide slavery phenomena, slaves worked for their captors, while others could buy their freedom. Chattel slavery in West Africa was different. The chattel slave trade in West Africa as was first initiated by Christian Portugal and Spain, who were then joined by many Christian European countries. Its victims became just "commodities", which were shipped to places thousands of miles away, where they were just "things" to be disposed of at any time and anyhow; their descendants also inherited their slave status.

When Christianity was introduced and a few schools were set up, the Guinea Coast women were excluded from formal education or learning how to read and write for a long time. Later on, those few females who had a limited formal education had to change their own ancestral names. They were required to take foreign Christian names from the Holy Bible, followed by their fathers' last names first, and then their husbands' last names when they married; this was in accordance with the European Christian marriage laws, as already explained.

Gradually, West African women came to be considered second-class human beings, like the women in the cultures of origin of these European Christian men who were the North Atlantic chattel slave traders, missionaries, and colonialists. The very serious question which humanity must now answer is: do modern civilized religious people treat women well?

The answer, paradoxically, is that chattel slave trading of young girls and young women is still taking place, right now in the 21st Century in the civilized Christian Western World, right under the noses of well-organized security establishments. For example, how many children go missing in the European Union every year?

Quite recently, sometime in 2014, I asked a woman from one of the Scandinavian countries about how modern women are treated in her country. She said:

> "Well, only a few weeks ago, hundreds of nursing mothers demonstrated right in the open in the city center of Copenhagen, by breast feeding their babies openly. Because nursing mothers cannot feed their tiny hungry babies, even discreetly, at places like public waiting rooms, bus and train stations, airports, restaurants and cafeterias, or department stores. In short, they cannot feed their babies anywhere outside their homes where men will see them. It does not matter how desperate and hungry the tiny baby is. Because men do not want to see such "indecent" scenes".(75)

This is only one example of women's ongoing situation in civilized Christian Europe: mothers are told, "Let your tiny babies starve until you get home". Such is civilization in Christian Europe today. There are numerous other problems for women in this so called "civilized" world. Many scholars today doubt the extent to which Western women have reached emancipation or complementary existence with their men. Men in ancient West Africa did not view women as sex objects, as men do in modern times in many parts of this world. During that period, a woman was valued as an equal, a mother and advisor and a loving wife, as well as a cornerstone for her community and for humanity.

Regarding the West African women's irreparable tragedy, I met many people during my travels conducting anthropological field research in West Africa, who argued thus:

> "First, regarding chattel slave trading, the so-called "primitive heathen people" did not ship their own people

to Europe for the "civilized" Christian Europeans to buy. Even if they had done that, these Christians should have stopped them. Second, the Christian European colonialists and missionaries built only a few schools for the locals, just to serve their own immediate needs. They could have built proper educational institutes to educate the natives properly, to enable them to build factories to process the tons and tons of gold, diamonds, and other precious metals, as well as huge amount of timber, they shipped back to Europe. They could have helped these West Africans to develop their economies. Much later on, tons and tons of cocoa beans were also shipped away to Christian Europe, but not one single chocolate factory was built to export ready-made chocolate. It was later on that some of these cocoa-producing countries took the initiative to set up a few small factories themselves.

"The Great Prophet Jesus Christ has a great message for humanity. That is, that there is a Creator God and that we must love our neighbors as ourselves, offering good service to our fellow human beings and forgiving those who treat us badly. Besides this wonderful message, Jesus also showed respect for women in the most unusual way. That was, He loved His mother Mary, showing her great attention and respect. To this day, the Christian World continues to show respect for "Mother Mary" in many ways. Therefore, the problem for the women in West Africa, as far as Christianization was concerned, was that Jesus Christ's message was introduced in the wrong way, as Christian Europe ignored the important natural position of women as foundation cornerstones for humanity on this earth.

"The real secret reason underlying these European Christians' presence in West Africa was their scramble for power to rule, as well as their obsession with material wealth. As the West African women were clever and powerful, the Europeans became afraid of them, and therefore silenced them forever."

Finally, during my Anthropological research work travels in some parts of West Africa, all the people I talked to about West African Women's everlasting calamity, people of both genders, of all ages, from different walks of life, of different cultures and religions, all agreed with one old man who once said to me that:

"CHRISTIAN EUROPE HAS TO APOLOGIZE TO THE WEST AFRICAN WOMEN OF TODAY, AS WELL AS TO WEST AFRICAN WOMEN'S DESCENDANTS IN THE AMERICAS AND THE CARIBBEAN!"

This should be, they argued, in the form of monuments erected in these former traders' capital cities, showing a "primitive", enslaved African nursing mother, with her baby hanging onto her dried-up empty breasts and her toddler clinging on to her legs, with the inscription:

TOPPLED CORNERSTONES, WE ARE SORRY!

Up to the present day, in this 21st Century, the huge "talking drums" of the Guinea Coast Africans are still echoing sympathy for the lost West African women:

**TOPPLED CORNERSTONES,
WE SYMPATHIZE WITH YOU!**

APPROXIMATE DATES FOR HUMAN EXISTENCE AND ACTIVITIES IN WEST AFRICA

39,000 BCE	Proof of human presence in West Africa's Savannahs
10,000 BCE	Organized human activities, as proved by studies of archeological records, started from this era
3,000 BCE	Igbo-Ukwu civilization begins
2,400-2,000 BCE	Jebel Uri, a city built in the Kanem-Bornu Empire, was one of the largest and most important cities built in West Africa
900 BCE-200 CE	Civilization in Nok, Southern Nigeria
300 BCE-900 CE	Various tribes migrate from the Nile Valley to West Africa
300 BCE-1239 CE	Ghana Empire
163 BCE-1463 CE	In the Mali Empire, the Keita Dynasty ruled for thirteen centuries, thus becoming one of the longest-ruling dynasties in the world
500 CE-1500 CE	In the Benin Empire, the Edo people constructed underground tunnels to connect villages
700 CE-1700 CE	The Empire of Kanem-Bornu
900 CE	The origins of the Hausa and Yoruba states
1054 CE-1591 CE	The rule of the Dia kings began in the new Songhay Empire

1076 CE	Beginning of the collapse of the Ghana Empire, due to the Almoravid Islamic wars
1200 CE	Ogiso rulers in the early state of Benin
1230 CE	The beginning of the rule of Mali's new king, Sundiata
1300 CE-1900 CE	Beginning of the Empire of Wolof (Senegal)
1305 CE	Ships were sent to explore the Americas by Mansa Abu Bakari II, who himself first sailed to Mexico in 1312
1310 CE-1491CE	Mande merchants make contact with Central America and the Caribbean
1400 CE	The Mossi states come into existence
1650 CE	The rise of the Fon state in Dahomey, as well as the early Bambara state of Segu

ILLUSTRATIONS

MAPS

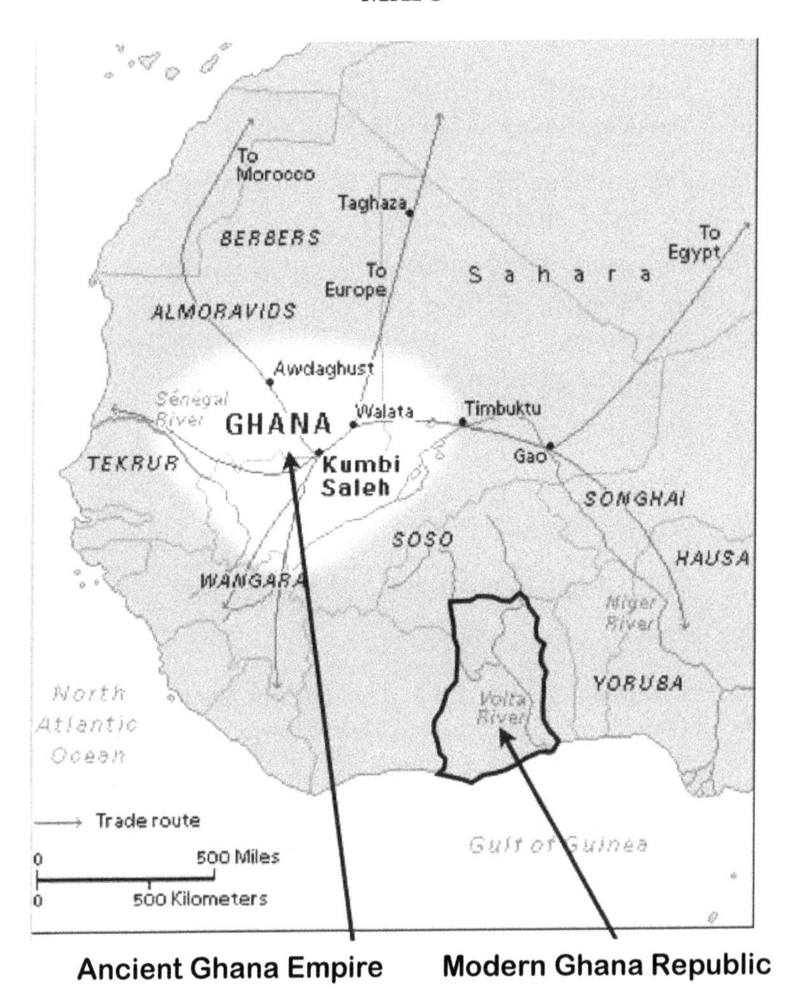

Ancient Ghana Empire and Modern Ghana Republic

NOTES AND AUTHORITIES CONSULTED

a. Notes

1. Knudsen, C. O. 2010. *The Theologian Slave Trader*. Dartford: Pneuma Springs Publishing. p. 16.
2. Trimingham Spencer, J., 1959. *Islam in West Africa*. Oxford: Clarendon Press. p.1.
3. Ogunleye, T., 1999. "Women in Ancient West Africa", in Vivante, B. (ed.), *Women's Roles in Ancient Civilizations: A Reference Guide*". Greenwood Publishing Group Incorporated. p.191.
4. *Ibid.*, p. 1.
5. *Ibid.*, p. 192.
6. *Ibid.*, p. 197.
7. Trimmingham Spencer, J., 1959, p. 1.
8. Ogunleye T., 1999, p. 191.
9. Knudsen, C. O., 1994. The Falling Dawadawa Tree: Female Circumcision in Developing Ghana. Højbjerg: Intervention Press. p. 26.
10. Ogunleye T., 1999, p. 191.
11. Abdurrahman Es Sadi, *Tarikh-es-Sudan* (History of the Sudan).
12. Ogunleye, T., 1999, p. 204.
13. Akosua Aidoo, A., 1981. "The Asante Queen Mothers in Government and Politics in the Nineteenth Century" in Steady, F. (ed.), *The Black Woman Cross-Culturally*. Cambridge, MA: Schenkman. p. 65.
14. Ogunleye, T., 1999, p. 211.
15. Ancient Oral History.

16. Ogunleye, T., 1999, pp. 211-212. See also: Hamdum, S. & King, N. 1994. *Ibn Battuta in Black Africa*. Princeton: Markus Weiner Publishers. pp. 37, 39.

17. In the "Twi" dialect, this is the name of the goddess who controls and protects earth and the various activities done on it, including farming.

18. The "Twi" word for the Creator God (Akan Oral History).

19. Akosua Aidoo, A., 1981, p. 65.

20. See Delphyne, F. A. 1991. *The Emancipation of Women*. Accra: Ghana University Press. p. ix.

21. Knudsen, C. O., 1994, pp. 26-27.

22. Ogunleye, T., 1999, p. 205.

23. Knudsen C. O., 2010, p. 28.

24. Ogunleye, T., 1999, p. 203.

25. Ancient Oral History.

26. Trimingham Spencer, J., 1959, p. 6.

27. Trimingham Spencer, J., 1955. *The Church and Islam in West Africa*. Edinburgh: SCM Press. p. 9.

28. Trimingham Spencer, J., 1959, p. 7.

29. *Ibid.*, p. 73.

30. *Ibid.*, p. 158.

31. Gansell, A. R., 2012. "Women in Ancient Mesopotamia." In James, S. L. & Dillon, S. (eds.), *A Companion To Women In The Ancient World*. Oxford: Blackwell Publishing. p. 23.

32. Marty, P. 1921. *Islam en Guinée*. Paris: Fouta-Djallon Editions. p. 373.

33. Trimingham Spencer, J., 1959, pp. 126-129.
34. Ogunleye, T., 1999, p. 213.
35. *Ibid.*, p. 214.
36. Trimingham Spencer, J., 1962, p. 32.
37. Ogunleye, T., 1999, p. 201.
38. *Ibid.*, p. 215. See Further Reading.
39. See Kalu, O. U. (ed.), 1980. *A History of Christianity in West Africa*. London & New York: Longman; Wiltgen, R. M., 1956. *Gold Coast Mission History, 1471 - 1880*; Baeta, C. G. (ed.), 1968. *Christianity in Tropical Africa*. London. pp. 34 - 56.
40. Knudsen, C. O., 2010, pp. 30, 31, 44.
41. *Ibid.*, pp. 31, 32.
42. Ward, W. E. F. 1958. *A History of Ghana*. London: Allen and Unwin. p. 34; Claridge Walton, W. 1915. *A History of the Gold Coast and Ashanti*, Vol. II. London: J. Murray.
43. *Ibid.*, pp. 64-69. See also Knudsen, C. O., 2010, pp. 16-18.
44. *Ibid.*, p. 21. See also Hansen, T. 1967. *Slavernes Kyst*. Copenhagen: Gyldendals. p. 23.
45. Ward, W. E. F., 1958, p. 414.
46. Knudsen, C. O., 2010, p. 65.
47. Hansen, T., 1967, pp. 193-200.
48. Knudsen, C. O., 2010, p. 86.
49. *Ibid.*, p. 25.
50. For more information, see Barbot, J. 1756. *A*

Description of the Coasts of North and South Guinea. London: A. & J. Churchill.

51. Ogunleye, T., 1999, pp. 190-191.
52. *Ibid.*, p. 202. Ward W. E. F., 1958, p. 308.
53. Ogunleye, T., 1999, p. 213.
54. Delphyne, F. A., 1991, pp. 14-21, 26, 36.
55. Trimingham Spencer, J., 1962, pp. 220-221.
56. See Trimingham Spencer, J., 1955.
57. Kalu O. U. (ed.), 1980, p. 163; Wiltgen, R. M., 1956; Baeta, C. G. (ed.), 1968, pp. 34-56
58. *Ibid.*, p. 215.
59. *Ibid.*, p. 216.
60. Ryder, A. F. C. 1969. "Portuguese Missions in West Africa." *Tarikh*, 3(1), 2-13.
61. An Oral History from Nana Kwaku Oware, a Divisional Chief of the Kingdom of Akyem Abuakwa, Gold Coast, who traded in gold with the European Colonialists just before 1850. However, this tradition was relaxed immediately after Gold Coast attained Independence in 1957.
62. Knudsen, C. O. 2000. The Patterned Skin: Ethnic Scarification in Developing Ghana. Højbjerg: Intervention Press. p. 92.
63. Check my website to see other books that I have written about my research work, including *The Falling Dawadawa Tree*: www.christianaknudsen.com
64. Kalu, O. U. (ed.), 1980, p. 309.
65. *Ibid.*, p. 3.

66. Gallagher, J. 1958. "Fowell Buxton and the New African Policy, 1838-1842." *Cambridge Historical Journal,* 10(1), 46 ff; Pinnington, J. 1969. "Church Principles in the Early Years of the Church Missionary Society: The Problem of the German Missionaries." *Journal of Theological Studies,* 20(2), 523-532.

67. See map of the old Gold Coast, showing ethnic Akan areas. Modern Ghana's population is 25.37 million, of which the Akan ethnic population is 11.5 million.

68. Dingwall, E. J. 2014. *Woman: An Historical, Gynecological and Anthropological Compendium. Vol. 1-111.* London: Butterworth-Heinemann; Knudsen, C. O., 1994, pp. 31-41, 124-127.

69. See Delphyne, F. A., 1991.

70. Knudsen, C. O., 2000, p.92.

71. BBC World Service: 2 August 2011; 21 August 2011; 13 September 2011.

72. For detailed information about the castles, forts and posts built on the Guinea Coast by European chattel slave traders, see Ward, W. E. F., 1958, pp. 414-418.

73. See Shepherd Verene, A. 1999. *Women in Caribbean History.*

74. Diop Chelkh Anta. 1987. *Black Africa: The Economic and Cultural Basis for a Federated State.*" Translated by H. J. Salemson. Trenton, NJ: Lawrence Hill Books. p. 33.

75. Denmark's DRTV1 report on 3 July 2014, "Aftenshowet", about the debate over the indecency of young mothers breast-feeding their desperately crying tiny babies at places where other people will see them, and arguments that, if such mothers need

to breastfeed their babies outside their homes, it has to happen at places where there are no people. An article about this debate can also be found in the Danish daily newspaper, "mx metro press", Copenhagen, 4 September 2014, p. 4.

b. Further Reading

1. Arhin, K. 1983. "The Political and Military Roles of Akan Women". In Oppong, C. (ed.), *Female and Male in West Africa*. London: Allen and Unwin.
2. Balander, G. 1970. *Sociology of Black Africa*. New York: Praeger Publishers.
3. Barbot, J. 1732. *A Description of the Coasts of North and South Guinea*. London: A. & J. Churchill.
4. Bosman, W. 1737. *Nauwkeurige beschryving van de Guinese Goud-Tand-en Slavekust*. J. Verheide.
5. Green-Pedersen, S. E. 1974. *Transactions of the Historical Society of Ghana*, Vol. 16. Accra: Legon University.
6. Hansen, T. 1987. *Slavernes Kyst*. Copenhagen: Gyldendals.
7. Hoxcer Jensen, P., Haar, L., Hahn-Pedersen, M., Jessen, K. U., & Damsgaard-Madsen, A. 1983. *Dansk kolonihistorie. Indføring og studier*. Aarhus; Aarhus Universitet.
8. Knudsen, C. O. 2010. *The Theologian Slave Trader*. UK: Pneuma Springs Publishing.
9. Knudsen, C. O. 1994. *The Falling Dawadawa Tree: Female Circumcision in Developing Ghana*. Aarhus: Intervention Press.

10. Rodney, W. 1969. "Gold and Slaves on the Gold Coast". *Transactions of the Historical Society of Ghana,* 10. 13-28.

11. Sørensen, H. E. 1992. Fridericus Africanus. Skaerbaek: Melbyhus.

12. Svane, F. P. A. 1748. *En Kort Sandfaerdig og Omstaendelig General Declaration*. Kobenhawn, The King's Library.

About Christiana Oware Knudsen

Christiana Oware Knudsen was born in the Gold Coast, now Ghana. As a young newly trained school teacher she met and married the Danish medical doctor, Peder K. K. Knudsen in Ghana in 1955. They had three children and then moved to Denmark. Christiana O. Knudsen holds a Cand. Phil. degree in Social Anthropology from the University of Aarhus, Denmark.

She carried out research and published books about Female Circumcision in developing Ghana, THE FALLEN DAWADAWA TREE in 1994, and Tribal Markings in Ghana, THE PATTERNED SKIN, in 1996. She has also done research into Distant Spiritual Healing as Complementary to medical health care, and was awarded a Ph.D. degree at Derby University, UK. in 2001. In 2008 she published a satire about some Danish holiday makers and the extraordinary problems they encountered due to their excessive materialism. In 2010, she published the controversial book, "THE THEOLOGIAN SLAVE TRADER".

Other Book(s) by Christiana Oware Knudsen

The Theologian Slave Trader ISBN 9781907728006
The Theologian Slave Trader explores the life of Fredericus Petersen, a mulatto adopted in 1710 by a Danish Lutheran Priest at Christiansborg Fort in what is now Ghana and who was subsequently brought back to Denmark as a teenager. Fredericus Petersen wrote a compelling autobiography which for many years has been largely ignored until now.

Lightning Source UK Ltd.
Milton Keynes UK
UKHW011836021020
370931UK00002B/801